# UNDERSTANDING

# FORESTS

OTHER BOOKS BY JOHN J. BERGER

*Nuclear Power: The Unviable Option. A Critical Look at Our Energy Alternatives* (Ramparts Press, 1976; Dell Books, 1977)

*Restoring the Earth: How Americans Are Working to Renew Our Damaged Environment* (Alfred A. Knopf, 1985; Doubleday Anchor Books, 1987)

*Environmental Restoration: Science and Strategies for Restoring the Earth* (ed.) (Island Press, 1990)

*Charging Ahead: The Business of Renewable Energy and What It Means for America* (Henry Holt and Company, 1997)

# UNDERSTANDING
## FORESTS

**A SIERRA
CLUB BOOK**

## JOHN J. BERGER

↩

The Sierra Club, founded in 1892 by John Muir, has devoted itself to the study and protection of the earth's scenic and ecological resources — mountains, wetlands, woodlands, wild shores and rivers, deserts and plains. The publishing program of the Sierra Club offers books to the public as a nonprofit educational service in the hope that they may enlarge the public's understanding of the Club's basic concerns. The point of view expressed in each book, however, does not necessarily represent that of the Club. The Sierra Club has some sixty chapters coast to coast, in Canada, Hawaii, and Alaska. For information about how you may participate in its programs to preserve wilderness and the quality of life, please address inquiries to Sierra Club, 85 Second Street, San Francisco, CA 94105. www.sierraclub.org/books.

LIBRARY OF CONGRESS CATALOGING-IN-PUBLICATION DATA

Berger, John J.
  Understanding forests / John J. Berger.
    p.  cm.
  Includes bibliographical references and index.
  ISBN 0-87156-420-3 (softcover)
    1. Forests and forestry — United States.  2. Forest ecology — United States.  I. Sierra Club.  II. Title.
SD143.B47    1998
333.75–dc21                      97–45867
                                      CIP

Design, composition, and production by BookMatters
Cover design by Amy Evans McClure

Printed on acid-free paper containing a minimum of 50% recovered waste paper of which at least 10% of the fiber content is post-consumer waste.

10 9 8 7 6 5 4 3 2 1

*To my children, Daniel and Michael—*
*May the forest practices we choose*
*assure splendid, healthy forests*
*for all future generations' enjoyment.*

Our current treatment of the forest is radical—
destruction of forest ecosystems for short-term benefits.
Herb Hammond, *Seeing the Forest among the Trees*

# CONTENTS

# Preface

Experience the majesty and beauty of wild forests. Walk in the cool, quiet grandeur of old growth far below its leafy canopies among the towering, furrowed trunks of massive ancient trees. Feel the spiky needles of spruce, the softness of fir, or the flattened leaf blades of coast redwood. Camp on an unspoiled stream bank beneath giant trees where the water is clean and cold enough for brook trout and salmon, and pure enough to drink. Sleep peacefully under a starry sky in the tranquility of unspoiled nature where neither the roar of traffic, the blare of electronic media, nor the artificial lights of human settlements intrude.

We desperately need places where these experiences are still possible. Wild forests represent the climax of millions of years of evolution. It is forest from which we came, forest that guided the evolution of our prehensile limbs and binocular vision, and forest that we must reenter from time to time if we are to keep in touch with some essence of our primal selves.

As conservationist John Muir pointed out a hundred years ago, wild places relieve the stress of urban living. They protect and renew us mentally and physically. We cannot rise to our full human potential without them. We must retain as much true forest habitat among us as we possibly can, or tomorrow we may have to spend thousands of dollars and travel thousands of miles to see a natural healthy forest. To some extent, that is already true. Nowadays we must go to Alaska or parts of Canada, for example, if we are to see large predators, such as grizzly, black bear, and wolf, in abundance. Undisturbed wild places are vanishing fast and are already all too rare, remote, and vulnerable.

With the loss of wild forests go opportunities for high-quality wilderness recreation, for scientific study, or for subsistence hunting, fishing, and gathering. But human gratification and the fulfillment of our immediate utilitarian needs are only two of the most obvious among myriad reasons for taking good care of forests. More fundamental reasons are that forests protect soil, water, wildlife habitat, climatic stability, and biological diversity. A healthy forest not only offers life forms of awesome size and age, such as incense cedar, bristlecone pine, and bull moose, but also harbors tiny organisms, such as Nelson's hairstreak, a delicate, rust-colored butterfly with inch-long wings that lives on incense cedar. Forests are also home to magnificent songbirds, such as the brilliant western tanager; astoundingly shaped and variegated mushrooms, such as the fluted white helvella; brilliant lilies, paintbrushes, columbines, and orchids; and fascinating insects, amphibians, mammals, and reptiles. Clearly, forests must be protected and restored for their intrinsic worth, apart from their beauty and value to us. Forests are complex ecological treasures that have a right to exist. We may use them, but no more ought to obliterate them than to demolish temples filled with rare illuminated manuscripts and priceless antiquities we scarcely understand.

After a clearcutting operation, dismembered remains of ancient trees lie strewn about, limbs and boughs shattered. The forest understory is crushed and uprooted, severed by roads, and scourged with skid trails. Exposed soil, churned and compacted, bakes dry in the sun. Wildlife is dead or has fled in terror.

Evidence of carnage is often scraped up and burned by timber companies eager to sterilize the scene, like orderlies in a bat-
tlefield surgical theater. Herbicide is sprayed. A single-species,
even-age tree crop is planted where the multispecies, multisto-
ried, uneven-age forest once stood. The best that can be hoped
for here is akin to a tree plantation—if the "reforestation" works
at all. The worst possibility is catastrophic erosion, loss of soil to
bedrock, polluted streams, parched springs, and wasteful rever-
sion of the land to an ecologically primitive, unproductive state.

Many well-meaning people, however, do not see the risks
nor even understand what forests are, much less the complexities
of their operation; which ones are rare or fragile; how we (and
wildlife) benefit from healthy forests; nor how old-growth
forests differ ecologically from second-growth. These folks typically do not recognize the consequences of forest destruction or
degradation, nor the immense difficulties in recreating authentic
forest on despoiled land. They will argue, for example, that ancient forests are "overripe" or "decadent" and that we must remove dead trees or fallen logs for the forest's own good, not re-
alizing that these natural elements—resources, actually—are
essential to the functioning of forest ecosystems.

I therefore wrote this book to explain how forests work, to
discuss the fate of forests, and to suggest principles for their
proper management. I believe that we can and must treat our
forests better than we have in the past; that wisdom and knowledge are needed to guide the protection and use of forests; and
that, with little effort, we, as consumers, can greatly reduce the
relentless demand for wood that drives deforestation.

Management practices on millions of acres of forest are in dispute today. Battles are raging from Maine to Alaska on the
ground, in the courts, in Congress, in state legislatures, and with
forestry boards. Many National Forest plans are due for review

in the final years of the 1990s. Forest controversies have engaged the attention of top political leaders, have leapt onto the front pages, and have even appeared on the evening news.

In 1996, a U.S. senator, a deputy secretary of the interior, and a state resources secretary engaged in high-profile negotiations with financier Charles Hurwitz and his Maxxam Corporation over the fate of the Headwaters Forest, the Earth's largest unprotected ancient redwood forest, located near Eureka, California. Thousands of demonstrators fervently protested Pacific Lumber Company's (PLC) logging plans for the 60,000-acre forest. (PLC is Maxxam's subsidiary.) Several protesters occupied illegal perches in the trees of the Headwaters to prevent logging. Others chained themselves to heavy equipment or barricaded logging roads. In the largest mass arrest in the forest protection movement's history, nearly a thousand people were arrested in a single 1996 Headwaters protest involving civil disobedience on Pacific Lumber land.

Even the president of the United States, the vice president, and senior cabinet officials have been drawn into forest controversies. In 1993, President Clinton convened a "forest summit conference" in Portland, Oregon, and personally helped negotiate an agreement to resolve forest conflicts in the Pacific Northwest, promising $1.2 billion in federal funds to retrain timber workers and restore forest land in return for an end to logging on the last remaining 6 million acres of old-growth forest and a reduction in the allowable cut in the region's National Forests.

Then, in 1995, with an ill-advised stroke of the pen, the president—after an earlier veto—signed a spending bill with an unrelated rider that released certain contested timber sales halted by previous court order and authorized "salvage logging" to begin—exempting those operations from all environmental and forest management regulations. (Salvage logging, properly conducted, is the removal of diseased, dying, and dead trees, but under the rider, timber companies and the Forest Service used salvage logging as a pretext to enter roadless old-growth wilderness and clearcut thousands of acres of perfectly healthy trees.)

The salvage-logging rider in effect created a loophole in environmental laws big enough to drive a logging truck through, and a federal court soon broadened the law's purview far beyond President Clinton's expectations. The president later admitted that signing the salvage-logging rider was a mistake. According to its critics' calculations, salvage logging under the rider may have cost taxpayers as much as a billion dollars in subsidies from the Forest Service to multinational timber firms before the rider expired at the end of 1996. Although the environmental community had strenuously opposed the president's decision to accept the salvage-logging rider in 1995, warnings went unheeded.

Late in 1996, a statewide referendum on clearcutting was held in Maine, where paper companies have ravaged the spruce and fir forests of the state's North Woods. The size of clearcuts was limited. Another well-publicized battle was fought the same year over logging by Louisiana Pacific Corporation in the Tongass National Forest in Alaska, where public timber was long being sold "below cost" to the giant timber company, which clearcut it on a monumental scale. (Below-cost sales are those in which the revenue received by the Forest Service does not even cover the costs it incurs to make the sale possible; such costs typically include road construction at taxpayers' expense to make timber removal possible. The Forest Service is in essence obliged to engage in below-cost sales because of the timber industry's political power.) Failing to obtain continued support for its activities in Congress, Louisiana Pacific decided to close its Tongass operation. Other smaller firms, however, are continuing to bid on and clearcut the old growth in the Tongass National Forest, largest of all our National Forests.

Abroad, battles against chainsaws and tractors are under way from Brazil to Indonesia, in order to prevent the destruction of tropical forests, and from the ancient Douglas fir forests of British Columbia to the boreal forests of the vast Siberian taiga, in order to protect northern temperate forests, too. These are just a few examples of important forest controversies flaring today as concerned citizens and interest groups respond to the worldwide assault on the Earth's forests.

What lies behind demonstrators' willingness to risk life and limb, fines and imprisonment, time and money, to stand between loggers' chainsaws and trees? Timber companies, forest workers, government officials, hunters, fishers, ranchers, hikers, campers, horseback riders, environmentalists, and ordinary forest users all have a huge stake in the outcomes of these confrontations. The global timber industry is a multibillion-dollar business with an insatiable appetite for wood and a powerful imperative to cut and process it at a profit. Tens of thousands of jobs depend directly on forests; millions of acres of land are affected by decisions about forest use. The economies of many towns depend on forest resources. A ban or sharp reduction in logging can force mill closures, eliminate jobs, devastate a tax base, and lead to the loss of community services. A prosperous local economy can be destroyed or whipsawed from boom to bust by forest abuse.

By contrast, forest protection and wise stewardship can lay the groundwork for a healthy, stable economy, as recreational, fish, and wildlife benefits from nondestructive forest use are generally far more valuable and far more enduring than revenue from one-shot clearcut logging operations. Brutal and short-sighted industrial forestry strip-mines forest capital and destroys forest assets rather than husbanding those resources so communities can enjoy forests' bountiful sustainable yields. Over time, consistent modest yields far exceed the spoils of greedy forest mistreatment.

The outcomes of forest controversies will affect far more than wallets and balance sheets. Forests are living museums and libraries of natural history. Many of our forests, such as the old-growth forests of California and the Pacific Northwest, are irreplaceable biological treasures that are the last refuges of threatened and endangered species, such as the marbled murrelet and the northern spotted owl. The way we resolve forest conflicts will largely determine the kinds of forests that our children will enjoy. Our decisions will respectfully preserve or despoil their natural heritage.

Forest management impacts also extend beyond the land to streams, rivers, lakes, groundwater, oceans, and even the air, through forest linkages to climate and effects on bird and insect life. Forests are crucial to the fate of dwindling stocks of wild fish, such as salmon, which spawn in forest streams and depend on healthy forests for their existence. Because of their importance in anchoring soil and absorbing rainfall, when forests are threatened, so are water supplies and water quality. Farmers and city dwellers alike thus depend on forests.

Forests saved from bulldozer and chainsaw can be lost imperceptibly due to air pollution, acid rain, and prolonged mismanagement. David Brower, the inspirational environmental leader, has called this piecemeal destruction of the natural world "a holocaust in slow motion." The pages that follow address both the catastrophic and the subtler, more insidious threats to forests in the United States and abroad. The goal of the book, however, is not mainly to chronicle the damage, but to explain its causes and consequences and to outline potent actions that can be taken to protect and restore forests.

Because this book is a brief, introductory overview, many topics are presented, and the treatment, even of critically important subjects, is greatly condensed. Subjects include forest ecology, economics, and management; forest and conservation history; forest laws and policies; tree planting as an aspect of forest restoration; timber practices; alternatives to wood; and tropical forests and international forestry issues.

The better one understands forest issues—that is, forest resources, what threatens them, and the obstacles to surmounting those threats—the greater are the chances of saving forests. Help from people of good will is urgently needed in that endeavor. Time is running out for many of the world's forests, but action now can still save some of them. That action will both improve our quality of life and protect Earth's magnificent but dwindling biodiversity. Future generations will cherish the gifts our labors protect today, long after the cut lumber would be forgotten.

# ACKNOWLEDGMENTS

I am indebted to many people for patiently sharing their knowledge and information with me. The list includes Mike Anderson, Louis Blumberg, Pam Brodie, Michael Goergen, Bruce Hamilton, Richard Harris, Robert Hrubes, Mike Landram, John LeBlanc, Tim McKay, Pam Muick, Walter Poleman, Charles Powell, Marvin Roberson, Kim Rodriguez, Larry Ruth, Walter Sullivan, and Judith Wait. I also want to acknowledge my teachers of environmental science at the University of California at Berkeley and at Davis. Among them are professors Michael Barbour, John Holdren, Allan Knight, Robert Robicheaux, and Michael J. Singer. I am particularly grateful to author Ray Raphael, forester Herb Hammond, and forest ecologist Chris Maser for their excellent books on forestry, which I have relied upon heavily in researching this volume.

I would also like to thank my wife, Nancy Gordon, for having somehow found the time during her busy schedule to keep my lunch box always filled as I set off for the office each morning; for reading and correcting this manuscript; and for having patiently and good-naturedly tolerated the many times I arrived home late from work or spent weekend hours in the office.

I am also grateful to Jim Cohee, my editor at Sierra Club Books, for his belief in this book, constructive criticism of the manuscript, and confidence and exemplary patience in awaiting its arrival. Finally, I would like to warmly thank Jim Levine, president of Levine♦Fricke♦Recon, Inc., for providing me with an office at Levine♦Fricke♦Recon on generous terms so that I could conduct research and write the first draft of this book in a congenial, professional setting. ↔

# CHAPTER I

# THE BOUNTEOUS FOREST

Our inability to see whole forests, to understand that
each structure has an indispensable function . . . is leading us towards forest destruction.

Herb Hammond, *Seeing the Forest among the Trees*

## What Is a Forest?

A forest is a totality of interdependent organisms
and their interrelationships, along with the place
where they exist, the physical structures that support them, and
the chemical compounds they use and exchange.

A forest is both the architecture or structure of an ecosystem
and the functions and interconnections of organisms within that
structure. Thus a forest is far more than a collection of trees.
Trees are simply a *feature* of the forest, albeit its most prominent
one. By contrast, a commercial forest is narrowly defined as land
capable of producing at least 20 cubic feet of timber per acre
per year.

Forests are actually assemblages of interrelated plants and
animals on terrain dominated by tall, woody vegetation. Many
scientists consider that a savanna—a grassland with widely
spaced trees—becomes a forest when at least 25 percent of its

surface is covered by tree crowns, though there is no universal agreement on that arbitrary number.

While this ecological notion of forest seems straightforward, in reality the word *forest* encompasses a large array of distinct forest types and infinite gradations between them. The eastern United States, for example, is home to such ecosystems as temperate beech-maple forest, oak-hickory forest, pine-oak forest, white-cedar swamp forest, and bald-cypress swamp forest, boreal bog forest and jack pine forest, as well as northern floodplain forest, southern riverine forest, and more. Before the virtual extinction of the native chestnut tree, the Northeast was also home to magnificent old-growth chestnut forests.

Western forests range from the spruce-hemlock temperate rain forests of the Northwest to the mixed pine and fir conifers of the Sierra montane forest, the aspens of the Rockies, and the Englemann spruce and bristlecone pines of the subalpine zones. Oak woodlands and the drier pinyon-juniper forests of New Mexico and Utah are some of the forest types that populate the interior. In the north are forests of white spruce, balsam fir, and pine, among others.

Even when dominated by a particular tree, the forest consists of many ecosystems and gradations between them. An oak-maple-beech forest, for example, may well include open glades, riparian areas, and rocky outcrops. Some stands of trees may be almost entirely oak, others predominantly maple, and still others an admixture, or a completely different community, due to soil, exposure, or elevational effects. Moreover, the forest may be in the process of invasion by new species, or some other change in the dominant tree type may be occurring.

Not coincidentally, the forest is a place of enormous complexity. In addition to trees, it includes soil, insects and other invertebrates, birds, mammals, amphibians, reptiles, herbs, grasses, shrubs, mosses, lichens, bacteria, fungi, and viruses. Competition, predation, respiration, photosynthesis, evolution, coalescence of new life, and dissolution of the old all go on simultaneously.

So elaborate and intricate are the linkages among parts of the forest that forest ecologist Chris Maser refers to the forest with awe as "a trillion-piece jigsaw puzzle." One way to think about forest, therefore, is as a plexus. Derived from the Latin word for "braid," *plexus* means an interlaced network of parts that together form a system. The forest plexus is thus a living, multidimensional web interconnecting various life forms and, through nutrient cycling, linking life with dead organisms and other mineral storehouses.

## Forest Products

Thanks to their complexity, natural forests are the source not just of wood but of an immense array of finished and raw products. Besides lumber for construction materials, veneer, and furniture, these include paper, adhesives, waxes, turpentine, polymers, gunpowder, medicinal herbs, perfumes, sachets, charcoal, mulch, fertilizer, musical instruments, and medicines such as taxol (from the Pacific yew) to treat cancer, quinine (from *Cinchona* tree species) to treat malaria, and digitalis (from foxglove) for heart disease. Of course, forests also provide raw logs, firewood, burls, ferns, mosses, lichens, flowers, mistletoe, wreaths, fruits, nuts, cones, incense, wild mushrooms, fish, and game.

In addition, compounds once synthesized exclusively by forest plants, animals, and microorganisms are today incorporated in a large number of commonly used medicines and have provided the chemical models and insights for countless pharmaceuticals worth tens of billions of dollars. Willow bark, for example, contains acetyl salicylic acid, the active ingredient in aspirin. Medicines originally derived from forests account for 40 percent of all commercially sold pharmaceutical preparations.

Apart from a cornucopia of forest products and the assorted economic benefits forests provide, forests also offer the world natural beauty, sacred places, and many invaluable ecological services, whose effects extend far beyond forest boundaries.

## Ecological Services

Through photosynthesis, forests both contribute oxygen to the atmosphere and remove carbon dioxide from it by storing carbon in the form of plant tissue. Forests thus tend to counterbalance global warming, which is intensified by increases in the concentration of atmospheric carbon dioxide.

Forests can affect climate locally and regionally through the release of moisture withdrawn from the soil by plant roots and then transported up stems or trunks to evaporate through leaves. Since atmospheric humidity is thereby increased, droughts may be reduced or prevented. Trees also can extract water from the air by their contact with low fog, causing moisture to condense on leaf surfaces and drip to the ground, where it can add substantially to total annual precipitation. Trees also moderate local temperature extremes and wind velocities by shading the ground and shielding it from storms and wind.

In addition to their influence on climate, forests purify water by filtering it through litter and soil. Much of the water we drink, either from surface or underground sources, comes from forested watersheds, including water that accumulated eons ago.

Forests also increase the amount of water reaching groundwater reservoirs by slowing the rate of surface runoff (which helps prevent floods) and thus increasing the percolation of runoff into the soil. This helps recharge deep groundwater reserves, raises the water table, and makes for more persistent stream flow during dry seasons, benefiting vegetation and wildlife.

More than half the water supply in the western United States flows from National Forests. Water from healthy forested watersheds can be used with minimal treatment by cities. When damaged forests can no longer perform their hydrological functions, expensive treatment plants may be needed, raising monthly water bills.

Forests build and protect the soil. Trees shelter soil and soil-building organisms from the effects of direct sun, wind, and precipitation. "Soil is the basis of the forest," says environmental leader David Brower. "We have to stop treating forest soil like dirt."

To forest ecologist Chris Maser, "Soils are the placenta that nurtures the forest." Soil and forest litter absorb rain like a sponge and release it to vegetation and groundwater slowly. By absorbing water from wet or waterlogged soils and releasing it into the air, forests can help stabilize soils.

Forests also are important contributors to the health of aquatic ecosystems by supplying leaves and other detritus to the water. This material serves as food for microorganisms, insects, and other life forms in the aquatic food web, ultimately feeding larger fish.

In addition to providing food, temperate forests also shade streams and rivers, keeping temperatures low enough for cold-water species. The effect of temperature on stream ecosystems is profound. Native fish and insects are temperature-sensitive. Cool water contains more oxygen than warm water, and oxygen is necessary for the survival, growth, and reproduction of aquatic organisms.

The favors granted by forests to streams and rivers are returned when flood waters crest overland, depositing nourishing sediment that enriches the land. The migration of salmon from the sea to forested headwater streams is yet another pathway by which valuable nutrients are returned to the land from the water.

Phosphorus, a nutrient that is relatively scarce in terrestrial ecosystems, is brought upstream from the ocean by the salmon, along with nitrogen and other elements. Some salmon are caught by bears or eagles; others simply die after spawning and are ingested by predators or scavengers. Nutrients from the fish, including the scarce phosphorus, are eventually returned to the soil as animal waste products. Author Robert Steelquist, in an article called "Salmon & Forests: Fog Brothers" in *American Forests,* refers to salmon as "swimming fertilizer sacks."

The normal healthy forest also stabilizes streams, faraway ocean beaches, and dunes by providing a profusion of fallen logs and branches as snags, logjams, and rootwads. These lodge in streams, creating pools and riffles and scouring the beds, introducing irregularities, or "heterogeneity," into the habitat. The wood may eventually be washed downstream, where it may become waterlogged and decompose in bays, oceans, and estuaries, providing habitat and food for bottom-dwelling and other marine and estuarine organisms.

Apart from the ecological services forests offer, they provide an abundance of opportunities for hiking, backpacking, camping, boating, fishing, skiing, nature observation, hunting, solitude, healing, and contemplation. They are sources of inspiration for art, literature, and music, as well as for spiritual guidance and self-discovery. Accurate forest description requires superlatives: forests contain the oldest as well as the tallest and the most massive living things on Earth. They are also the most diverse ecosystems in species per acre, especially when soil microorganisms are included.

## Forests, Biodiversity, and Endangered Species

Throughout the world, forests are home to many indigenous peoples. Over thousands of years, these local stewards have often acquired sophisticated ecological knowledge of their forests and have developed countless uses for the forest plant and animal products they harvest. To destroy or gravely damage forests not only may physically or culturally annihilate native peoples, but can lead to the loss of traditional ecological lore invaluable for forest management.

Forests are reservoirs of genetic diversity. They contain more species than any other ecosystem on Earth and are like a library of genetic information that can be used by species through time to adapt to changing environmental conditions. Genetic diversity, as restoration consultant Mary Lee Guinnon puts it, is a species' "bag of tricks," which the species uses to cope with whatever condition the environment presents. Maintenance of genetic diversity enables a species to improve its fitness and hence its chances of survival in response to altered environmental conditions. Depriving an ecosystem of its diversity therefore robs it of its ability to redesign itself by outfitting itself with better-adapted parts.

Healthy natural forests are templates that can be used as models for the human repair of damaged ecosystems. Maser refers to forests as repair manuals or spare-parts catalogs. When part of a degraded forest ecosystem is missing—when a species has become locally extinct, for example—species can be transplanted to the affected site from a healthy forest.

As existing forests, new and old, are stressed by pollution and climate change, we will need everything that nature has to teach us about repairing damaged forests and about reconstructing new ones. Ecologist Aldo Leopold once said, "The first rule of intelligent tinkering is to save all the parts." Ancient forests are not only valuable laboratories for the scientific study of forest processes, such as succession, and the evolution of species, but they are at once blueprints and live-action instructional videos for restoring forests.

Wild forests are living laboratories for studying how the natural processes of ecosystem assembly and evolution operate. Since forests differ from youth to old age, we need to protect and conserve diverse natural forest communities of all types and ages, from old growth to young forests, to assure ourselves adequate learning opportunities. The lush Appalachian cove forest with its white basswood, tuliptree, and fragrant magnolias, has different lessons to offer us than do the pine barrens of New Jersey.

The value of forests as storehouses of genetic information is not limited to being a species repository—either for warehousing living curiosities or for assuring a reserve of variability that enables natural ecosystems to adapt to environmental change. Genetic material from wild plants is also of incalculable economic value for improving the resistance of domestic crops to pests and disease, potentially avoiding billions of dollars in crop losses or diminished productivity.

Timber companies have been slow to recognize that the multiplicity of forest life forms constitutes what Maser wisely calls "the forest's immune system." Within the healthy forest's great diversity of interconnected organisms reside life forms—including birds, insects, and pathogens—that can serve the forest as white blood cells serve a body. These forest organisms are available to proliferate when needed to deter, mitigate, or cure imbalances in the relative sizes of populations of species. We call these imbalances epidemics or pest outbreaks.

Variegated forest types are habitats for diverse sensitive, threatened, and endangered species. When we destroy old-growth forests, for example, we are signing death warrants for such endangered species as the northern spotted owl and the marbled murrelet. Other endangered, threatened, or sensitive species that thrive in old growth are the red tree vole, the red-cockaded woodpecker, and the northern flying squirrel. Providing habitat for increasingly hard-pressed species is thus another ecological service forests provide.

Unfortunately, Congress has often not been in the vanguard of endangered species protection efforts. For example, the Republican-dominated 104th Congress passed a one-year moratorium in 1995 prohibiting the listing of additional species under the federal Endangered Species Act of 1973 in order to obstruct its implementation by federal agencies. Republicans in Congress tried to nullify and undermine the act, both by attempting to increase the difficulty of listing endangered species for protection and by trying to strike a key provision of the law that protects the habitat of an endangered species from destruction. Yet even under the law as now written, it is already so difficult to get a species on the Endangered Species List that some species die or are irrevocably set on the path to extinction before they can be listed.

## Forest Processes

How do forests manage to deliver their broad range of services and goods? The answer lies in the complex way in which forests capture, transform, and exchange energy. An understanding of these processes and other fundamental aspects of forest ecology is the foundation upon which sound forest policy must rest. By contrast, using economics and politics bereft of ecology as the basis of forest policy is a prescription for disaster. Therefore the following overview of the basic principles of forest ecology serves as a prelude to the discussions of forest management practices in later chapters.

Energy enters the forest as light. The forest captures this solar energy input within its leaves and uses it there to combine carbon dioxide taken from the air and water drawn from the soil to produce plant tissue. The entire process, called photosynthesis, is basic to all forest ecosystems.

Through photosynthesis, the forest provides oxygen to the atmosphere and participates in the perpetual global cycling of nutrients and moisture among air, bodies of water, soil, and plants. Meanwhile, forest plant roots extract minerals from soil and rock, incorporating these elements into plant tissues.

Tree leaves, stems, branches, roots, trunks, fruits, nuts, berries, pollens, and nectars feed a vast array of consumers, from tiny spores of leaf rust and leaf-cutter ants to moose that browse on leaves and twigs.

When dead or dying plant tissues, such as bark and tree trunks, fall to earth, they are broken down by organisms whose specialty in life is decomposition. Mushrooms, other fungi, bacteria, termites, and beetle larvae feed on the decaying wood. In doing their job, these decomposers help produce soil and perform critical nutrient cycling functions.

For its part, soil nourishes forest plants, supports microorganisms, provides habitat for animals, and catches, retains, and filters water, which flows through it to feed plants or percolate into underground flows known as aquifers. These underground reservoirs may discharge water to the surface in springs or flow directly into streams and rivers.

At first glance, the forest may appear simple and virtually empty. Much of the forest's life occurs underground and is therefore invisible to us as we stand above it. Billions of organisms—from yeast and fungi to moles, voles, shrews, salamanders, worms, beetles, spiders, mites, centipedes, millipedes, snails, and slugs—all are busy underfoot in the leaf litter and the organic layers of soil. All actively process nutrients and make them available to higher plants and other organisms. Subterranean life helps to create the soil and exudes compounds that bind soil particles together into useful little clumps called aggregates, which retain nutrients against leaching by rainfall.

The roots of many tree species are coated and interpenetrated with fungi known as mycorrhizae. These intimate associates are fed by the roots and in return offer the roots some protection against root disease, stimulate root tip growth, and greatly facilitate nutrient uptake. About 90 percent of all plants are thought to have mycorrhizae. Mycorrhizae send fungal filaments called hyphae into the surrounding soil, from which they transport nutrients to the roots, which provide the fungi with sugars in return.

The hyphae thus connect the roots both to the soil and to other mycorrhizae. Exudates from roots and hyphae along with sloughed organic matter support a complex community of soil organisms that include bacteria, protozoa, and invertebrates. Not surprisingly, many mycorrhizae improve seedling growth and survival dramatically. Some trees, such as pines, grow on nutrient-poor soil and *require* mycorrhizae.

Plant roots hold forest soil in place and in turn build more soil when they die and decompose, opening channels for water and air to enter soil. Masses of interwoven hyphal filaments known as mycelium are pervasive in the soil. Without their presence and activity, soil would eventually become a dusty or sandy mass of unconsolidated particles that could be easily blown away by wind or swept away by water.

As if trees knew how important soil is to the forest, they safeguard it in various ways. Trees shelter soil from the pounding of falling rain droplets and the harsh drying of wind and full sunlight. As leaves reduce droplet velocities, they also contribute nutrients leached by the rain from the leaf surface to the soil. Fallen leaves, branches, and trunks further slow the overground passage of water, increasing the seepage (infiltration) of water into the ground.

Although a forest appears static to the casual observer, the forest is cycling nutrients and moisture in complex, never-ending interchanges from the air, water sources, and soil into and among the forest organisms and back.

To manage this complex flow of material and energy, the

forest must be information-rich—that is, well stocked with a diversity of organisms. The information is packed in the coded genetic material—vast libraries of information—stored inside each cell of each forest organism. The encoded information guides the development of the multiplicity of organisms interacting in the forest ecosystem.

The forest is also organized in other respects. One aspect of its physical organization is the forest's architecture. Most multispecies forests are physically stratified into layers. Tall trees form the upper canopy, and shorter subcanopy trees, perhaps black cherry or dogwood, form a second layer. Shrubs, perhaps rhododendrons or elderberry bushes, fit themselves in underneath and among the trees; vines climb the trees or grow close to the ground; and wildflowers, herbs, and occasional outcrops of grass hug the ground.

Another important aspect of the forest's organization is the forest food web, or food pyramid. The web is based on the autotrophs—plants, such as algae, which manufacture their own food from sunlight and inorganic material. Autotrophs are consumed by heterotrophs, literally "other-eaters," which do not perform photosynthesis themselves, but survive by assimilating other organisms. Feeding is an organized activity, with herbivores, carnivores, omnivores, and detritivores each specializing (or generalizing) in their particular types of food.

## Patterns of Change Through Time

Each forest type has one or more characteristic developmental sequences or stages, known collectively as succession, by which the forest becomes established in its environment. In this process, the forest adapts to the environment and simultaneously adapts the environment to itself.

All the while, the successional process increases the complexity and the nutrient capital of the forest ecosystem. Nature's own system of crop rotation and natural fertilization meanwhile ensures that different nutrients and vertical soil strata (known as soil horizons) are used by forest organisms.

Like all ecosystems, forests are ever-changing. The patterns of change, however, are predictable only over large areas and long periods of time as forest ecosystems respond to natural disturbances. These include fires, earthquakes, windstorms, avalanches, landslides, floods, diseases, insect plagues, invasive plants, and the effects of grazers and browsers.

The advance and retreat of glaciers provide an extreme example of successional processes. As a glacier retreats, soil and plants are removed, often leaving only scraped rock and unconsolidated mineral substrate (such as sand and gravel). These materials are low in organic matter and lack structural complexity and stability. Willows and alders might be the first trees to establish on this rugged, difficult terrain.

Pioneer plants, such as alders, lupine, and ceanothus, contain nitrogen-fixing bacteria in nodules on their roots. These bacteria enrich the soil by removing molecular nitrogen from the air and incorporating it in the soil in soluble forms suitable for plant root uptake. Pioneers also stabilize bare soil, provide shade, reduce moisture loss, and sometimes offer young trees protection against certain insects.

Once the soil has been improved by these pioneers, other plants can become established in their turn. This process continues until a dynamically stable state has been reached in which no further broadscale species replacements are likely—until the next major disturbance, such as a forest fire, again upsets the forest's equilibrium.

Wild forests periodically and naturally have wildfires. These fires play important ecological roles in forest ecosystems and succession. Woody debris on the forest floor is consumed as flames scorch the ground, preventing fuels from accumulating in sufficient quantities to produce hotter and more damaging blazes.

Fires are one of nature's ways of cleansing the forest of dead and dying material, opening cones and other seed stores to release seed, removing insects and disease, releasing nutrients, and —through the patchy nature of most periodic burns—introducing additional habitat heterogeneity. A species' degree of susceptibility to fire influences its place in a forest's pattern of succession and may determine whether it dominates or relinquishes a site to another species.

The complexity of the natural forest's biological programming ensures that forces needed to repair the damage done by fire will be set in motion by the fire itself. For example, fire consumes organic litter on the forest floor, and while it releases nutrients in the form of ash, it also oxidizes nitrogen, which may be in short supply following a fire. Fortunately, the ash raises the soil's alkalinity, thereby improving its habitability by nitrogen-fixing bacteria that can restore nitrogen to the ecosystem.

Plants that are able to thrive on bare ground, or in disturbed areas, sprout after fires and begin the forest repair process. These pioneer species generally have rhizobium nodules of nitrogen-fixing bacteria on their roots, so they are soon adding large amounts of soluble nitrogen back into the soil. The new roots also hold the soil against erosion and break up compaction. Then, as the pioneer plants themselves shed body parts, they begin building a new supply of organic materials in the soil to replace those consumed by the fire.

When fire is long delayed, fuel accumulates, so that the inevitable fire will be an inferno. It climbs up tree trunks as if ascending a ladder and burns off tree crowns, killing the trees instead of just singeing the bark. Because of the intense heat, the soil may also be damaged. It may form a crust that resists water, delays forest recovery, and leads to erosion. For this reason, forest managers must be prepared to introduce fire as needed in forests where fuel buildup is no longer properly regulated by natural forces.

Many of the problems forest managers face today in National Forests, National Parks, and on private lands stem from the ecological ignorance that has guided decades of federal, state, and private fire-suppression policy. Huge buildups of fuel in many forests today threaten some forests and will necessitate expensive remedial control burns.

However, in other areas, Forest Service and timber company ignorance and indifference to the role played by a broad diversity of organisms in forests has led to the excessive removal of brush, downed wood, and snags (standing dead trees) that provided habitat for beneficial insects, birds, and mammals, which keep forest diseases and infestations from reaching epidemic proportion. Removal of these forest integuments—often accompanied by herbicide application—coupled with the decisions by industrial foresters to replace natural multiage, multispecies, multilayered canopies of trees with single-age, single-species stands of commercial timber, has left woods susceptible to ruinous plagues of bark beetles, budworms, and vectors (organisms that transmit pathogens).

Instead of heeding these outbreaks as warnings to begin reestablishing forests or to begin adopting sustainable forest policies for the future, commercial timber managers typically have resorted to massive applications of pesticides. Over several decades, millions of pounds of toxic chemicals that often endanger both nontarget species and water quality have been sprayed over millions of forest acres. While these treatments temporarily address the symptoms of forest imbalance, they do nothing fundamental to redress it, and thus the imbalance generally reappears in another guise, which may be misinterpreted by industrial timber managers as yet another reason for chemical control technology.

In our hubris, we have delivered multiple insults to forests by trying to manage them without conforming our actions to the principles of forest ecology. To the extent that these insults are unintentional, their common wellspring is ignorance. "Of all the myriad interdependent relationships in the forest," writes Herb Hammond in *Seeing the Forest among the Trees*, "we are aware of only a few. Ignorance coupled with technological prowess makes human alteration of the forest ecosystem very risky."

## Acid Rain and Ozone as Disrupters of Forest Processes

Forests are at risk not only from specific actions taken by forest managers and timber companies extracting timber on the ground, but from global environmental problems created by industrial and energy policies. Air pollution created by heavy industry, fossil-fueled power plants, and internal combustion engines produces oxides of sulfur and nitrogen that form nitric and sulfuric acid in the atmosphere. Carbon dioxide from natural and human sources also combines with atmospheric moisture to produce carbonic acid. All these acids naturally tend to acidify precipitation.

Airborne acids eventually fall out of the atmosphere in the form of acid rain, sleet, snow, or particulate deposition. They also hover in the atmosphere as acid fog, corroding high-elevation forests. Acid precipitation harms forests both through direct contact with trees and other plants as well as through indirect effects of the acids on soils. The effects on forests differ from forest community to community, tree species to species, and ecosystem to ecosystem, because of the great variations that occur in soil and vegetation, but the price is steep. Forest damage from acid rain costs the world tens of billions of dollars a year ($30 billion a year in Europe alone).

Not only are some of the effects of hyperacidity on soil cumulative, but they are also exacerbated by other potent pollutants, especially ozone, which sickens and yellows leaves, and by environmental stresses that can weaken a tree's resistance to pests and diseases. The overall result may be to reduce tree growth and productivity, physically damage leaves, cause premature leaf fall, inhibit reproduction, alter species composition, increase susceptibility to diseases or insects or climatic stress, and increase mortality.

Whereas at high concentrations, acid rain can damage plant leaves, shoots, cuticle (a protective waxy coating), and stomata (leaf pores through which plants breath), the most serious threat from acid rain appears to be the long-term cumulative effects on soil and aquatic ecosystems, particularly lakes, where the acid may accumulate, eventually killing aquatic life.

While some forest soils have a natural ability to neutralize acids, other soils are highly susceptible. In the susceptible forest, acid precipitation increases soil acidity, and toxic sulfate and nitrate ions build up. Soil changes then result in the "mobilization" of toxic aluminum and iron ions in soluble form from the soil. These heavy metals are then thought to be preferentially taken up by tree roots, inhibiting the uptake of the calcium and magnesium essential for growth. The latter two elements are also made soluble by acids, but then are leached from the soil at an accelerated rate. These processes may be responsible for slowing tree growth.

## Genetic Engineering and Forest Resilience

Timber companies frequently use trees cloned from identical genetic stock in converting forests into tree plantations. This genetic engineering exposes such plantations to the risk of future extinction. Natural forests, with their diverse genetic makeup, have an inherent capacity to adapt to long-term environmental change. The greater a species' natural variation, the greater the range of responses it can make to the forces of natural selection, and the greater the probability of it producing a "fit" individual, relative to its environment.

Trees of a species "propose" offspring, and subsequently the environment "disposes," deciding each offspring's fate based on whether or not it is suited to the fluctuating range of environmental conditions that determine its survival, such as temperature and moisture patterns. Because the variability of the cloned trees is far more limited than that of the natural forest population, the chances of the cloned population's *in*ability to adapt over long periods of time to changed conditions—and hence the chances of extinction—are much greater.

If climate warms dramatically in the next fifty to a hundred years, as climatologists throughout the world fear, the genetic variability of natural tree populations may be required if trees are to successfully "propose" genetically modified future generations that are better adapted to the new climatic conditions and altered fire regimes that go with them.

No one knows how millions of acres of genetically homogeneous trees will fare when exposed to these new stresses. By the time we can answer this question with confidence, it may be too late to do much about it.

# THE FOREST RESOURCE

A fallen tree is literally the soil for future generations of forests.

Herb Hammond, *Seeing the Forest among the Trees*

## Kinds of Forests

The world's forests can be classified according to their site, vegetation, general location, and other characteristics. For example, forests are broadly classified into northern or boreal, central, southern, tropical, interior, coast, montane, and subalpine types. For vegetational classification, forests are grouped by species composition. Vegetational composition ranges from pure stands of one tree species to various mixtures, such as oak-gum-cypress or aspen-birch. Specific understory plants are generally found in association with the different forest types.

Principal aspects of a site used for forest classification are the nature and depth of forest soil and litter, location, elevation, slope, temperature, and precipitation. Climate and soils are the principal overarching determinants of forest type, along with the later influence of fire, competition from other plants, and predation from animals. Since individual trees, once established, cannot move themselves from unfavorable sites, they must adapt

or die where they stand. Silvics is the study of how site characteristics and other environmental factors affect forests.

The two main forest types are those comprised of the needle-leafed and the broad-leafed trees. The broad-leafed species
are almost all deciduous trees, such as hazel, beech, and
sycamore, which loose their leaves every autumn. To confuse
matters, however, some broad-leafed trees are also evergreen
(nondeciduous), including the California live oak, the Pacific
madrone, the California bay laurel, and many tropical trees. Not
coincidentally, evergreen broad-leafed trees are found in temperate or tropical areas where frost is absent or infrequent.

The northern evergreens, such as spruce, pine, cedar, juniper,
and yew, are almost all needle-leafed. (An exception, the tama-
rack [American larch], is a needle-leafed deciduous tree.) Evergreens are generally adapted to colder climates with short growing seasons: Resinous compounds in the stems and leaves protect
evergreens against frost, much like antifreeze. Therefore, even in
cold climates, evergreens can maintain their needles year-round
to conserve the energy that otherwise would be required to replace their leaves each year.

Particular forest types are found in zones determined largely
by climate, as manifested in precipitation and temperature. (Climate also influences soil formation.) Altitude exerts a major influence on local climate, so forest zones correspond to changes
in altitude much as they do to the influence of latitude. Cooler
mountain regions, even in middle and southern latitudes, are
populated by cold-tolerant conifers.

Pure coniferous (cone-bearing) forests of fir, pine, spruce,
and larch grow in high, subpolar northern latitudes. These are
known as taiga forests and tend to have poor, shallow soils and
short, small-girth trees. By contrast, the moist, temperate conifer
forests, such as those on the U.S. west coast (from Alaska to central California) and inland to the Rockies, produce thick soils,

huge trees, and dense understory growth, replete with mosses and ferns. These ecological characteristics develop in response to the voluminous annual precipitation and milder weather, with a longer growing season.

Trees of the moist, temperate forest include Sitka spruce, western red cedar, western hemlock, Douglas fir, and redwood. Because conifers grow rapidly, they are usually used for reforestation in North American commercial forestry. These quickly grown softwoods, however, have wider growth rings and more sapwood and tend to warp and twist in drying more than mature old-growth timber. (This renders the immature softwood unsuitable for uses such as musical instruments that demand high-quality wood, and less suitable for construction, where strong, straight lumber is required.)

Immediately to the south of the pure coniferous forests in the Northern Hemisphere are transitional forests of mixed broad-leafed trees commingled with coniferous species. In the eastern United States, these forests include sugar maples, yellow birches, and American beech, interspersed with white pine and eastern hemlock, two conifers. Still farther south in the temperate zone, the conifers become sparser and eventually disappear, giving rise to forests comprised entirely of broad-leafed deciduous trees. Examples include eastern hardwood forests of beech-maple or maple-basswood and oak-hickory forests with their northern red oaks, scarlet and white oaks, and bitternut, shagbark, and pignut hickories.

Moving into the warm temperate latitudes, a gradual shift occurs in forest type to broad-leafed evergreens. These trees are dominant in tropical forests, which are extremely rich in species diversity. While northerners may think of all tropical forests as undifferentiated jungle, the tropics actually have very distinctive forest types, including equatorial rain forest, dry tropical forest, monsoon forest, mangrove forest, montane forest, and others, each with unique ecological features and communities of species. In addition to the widely distributed forest types, there are isolated and rare forest forms. The pygmy forests of coastal California, for example, are created by unique soil conditions; swamp forest and palm oases, too, result from unique hydrologic conditions.

## Ancient Forests

No one single characteristic defines an ancient forest or old-growth forest. The two terms are roughly synonymous, although "ancient" is more applicable to forests of great antiquity, with some trees many hundreds or thousands of years old, whereas an old-growth stand might be a "mere" 200 years in age in some forest ecosystems. When one says "old growth," the image that pops into mind is a stand of ancient giant sequoias, some more than 2,000 years old, with trunks large enough at the base for a car to drive through. Red cedar, Alaska yellow cedar, and bristlecone pine, however, get even older than redwood—3,000 years, 3,500 years, and more than 4,600 years, respectively.

The presence of large, old trees is not sufficient to qualify a site as an old-growth forest. David Middleton, writing in *Ancient Forests: A Celebration of North America's Old Growth Wilderness*, defines old-growth forest as "a structurally complex forest, hundreds of years old, that has not been directly altered by humans." That may be an apt definition if "alteration by humans" means the influence of industrialized society, but the definition ignores the fact that old forests were typically very much influenced (over long periods of time) by the activities of their aboriginal human inhabitants, especially their regular use of fire to manage forests. One need not withhold "old growth" designation from forests just because they were profoundly influenced by aboriginal peoples: humans, too, are part of nature and forest ecosystems.

By contrast, the words "structurally complex" *are* key to defining "old growthness." Complexity is expressed as variations in size, shape, age, and species—of other forest organisms as well as trees. Patchiness in the distribution of vegetation is another manifestation of complexity, as is the presence of a multilevel forest canopy rather than a homogeneous monolayer.

For a coniferous forest, the four main distinctive structural characteristics that develop over time and convert it to an old-growth ecosystem are: (1) presence of the multilevel forest canopy, (2) large, old living trees [large for the site and old for the species], (3) dead standing trees (snags), and (4) downed trees. In an insightful comment, holistic forestry expert Herb Hammond observes, in *Seeing the Forest among the Trees,* that "ancient forests seem to embody all aspects of the various phases of a forest," meaning that shrubby forest openings, young saplings, and mature, dying, and dead trees are all simultaneously present.

In addition to the four basic old-growth attributes mentioned, an old-growth forest exhibits wide variation in tree size and age and irregular breaks in the canopy caused by broken or fallen trees. These breaks allow light to penetrate to the forest floor and provide growth opportunities for young trees.

Each of the components of the old-growth ecosystem has important functions that help sustain the forest as a whole. For example, large, downed logs decay slowly on the forest floor and release their stored nutrients over periods of up to 400 to 500 years. During that time, they build soil fertility, provide food and shelter to numerous organisms, offer rooting media for new trees and other plants, slow surface runoff, trap and collect soil and nutrients, and, after being honeycombed by bark beetles and other wood borers, serve as spongy water-storage tanks for forest life during seasonal dry spells.

While it may appear forlorn and scraggly, the snag is actually, in Middleton's words, "an animal apartment house" that provides nesting, roosting, feeding, and denning opportunities to lots of species for many generations during the century or so that it may remain upright. The old-growth forest has an abundance of snags compared to a younger forest and also contains a relatively large amount of fallen wood. The dead, dying, and wounded trees that provide variation and irregularities within the forest are produced over centuries or millennia by the accumulated effects of disturbances, such as storms, wind, lightning, floods, fires, landslides, avalanches, insects, other pests, and even damage by birds.

Along the Pacific coast, the remaining uncut but rapidly vanishing old-growth forest is distributed from northern California to Alaska. Redwood–Douglas fir old growth grows as far north as Oregon. Douglas fir ranges into Washington, and Sitka spruce–western hemlock old growth can grow from northern Oregon to British Columbia and Southeast Alaska. The Pacific Coast ancient forest contains other large and impressive trees, such as the grand, noble, and Pacific silver fir.

Inland old growth and native forest are also found in Montana, Idaho, Colorado, Wyoming, Arizona, and New Mexico. Despite its value and scarcity, approximately 2 to 3 billion board feet of old-growth timber—60,000 to 100,000 acres—are still being cut annually in the Northwest, the Southwest, the northern Rockies, and the Tongass National Forest of Alaska.

Of the 850 million acres of original native forest in the lower continental United States at the time of the first European settlements, little ancient or "virgin" forest still survives. At best, only a few percent of the original forest has escaped the lumberman's ax and saw, and only 10 million acres of old growth are protected from cutting nationwide. As for Pacific Coast old-growth forest, well over 90 percent has been logged, and for some desirable species, the loss of old growth has been much greater. If current logging rates were to continue, all remaining unprotected Pacific Coast old growth would be gone in thirty years or so. Less than 2 percent of the original 2 million acres of redwood old growth are currently protected from logging, according to Middleton.

Vestigial as it is, however, most of the remaining old growth in the United States is found in the Pacific Northwest. Throughout the eastern United States, less than 1 percent of the old growth has been saved—probably less than a million acres—and it is found mostly in the Great Smoky Mountains and the Adirondacks. Apart from the Adirondacks and Smokies, most of the rest of the enormous eastern forest was logged and cleared at one time. The old growth left in the East is generally limited to only a few relatively small sites—25 acres here, 50 acres there. Some magnificent trees do remain, however, such as a stand of 1,700-year-old bald cypress on the Black River of Cape Fear, North Carolina.

Population growth and demand for "natural areas" from an increasingly urbanized populace are putting severe pressure on old growth as well as on forests of all types, but people are especially drawn to old-growth forests precisely because they are our last and most impressive examples of wild forest. Unless we retain these ancient forests and enhance existing second growth, we risk subjecting our healthy remnant forests to degradation from overuse and overexploitation. Through the cumulative impacts of their numbers, hordes of well-meaning, admiring people will nonetheless gradually destroy the objects of their affection, shattering wilderness tranquility. In addition, were we to reserve only a few examples of old growth, chances are most Americans would find these ancient forests remote and expensive to reach. We therefore need to maintain as many geographically dispersed and representative samples of our original forests as we can to help assure their accessibility and to minimize the ecological fragmentation of our remaining forests.

Timber interests and their allies have often made the bogus argument that because "trees are a renewable resource," cutting old-growth forest is a perfectly acceptable and harmless activity. Usually it *is* possible to replant trees after a forest has been clearcut. And, in due time, some of these trees *will* grow large. Seldom, however, do logging companies really make an effort to recreate the ecosystems they cut. And, even if they did, the history of modern industrial forestry is far too short for us to have demonstrated an ability to recreate old-growth forest conditions. These may include tons of mycorrhizae and epiphytes per acre (in a Northwest ancient forest, for example), nitrogen-fixing lichens, insects and birds for pollination, snags for habitat, and ancient, downed "nurse logs" for shelter, habitat, water management, and soil building.

"Old growth soil with untold thousands of organisms is the most biologically rich part of the ancient forest," notes Hammond. But without the diversity and complex interactions of the fully developed old forest, soil fertility will not recover to its antecedent condition after logging. With simplification of the forest by industrial forestry, and with habitat fragmentation caused by large clearcuts, forest genetic diversity, soil fertility, and water-holding ability will all decline, and forest life will not be as vigorous or robust as in a natural old-growth forest. In permitting our scarce remaining old-growth ecosystems to be destroyed, we may thus lose links in the great chain of forest life that is essential to the recreation of future forests.

# CHAPTER 3

# WHERE HAVE ALL THE FORESTS GONE?

There is no clear institutional leadership on forest issues at the global level.

*World Resources 1994–1995:*
*A Guide to the Global Environment*

## Lessons from History

The early European arrivals in North America acted as if the continent's forests, wildlife, fish, and soil were limitless and impervious to abuse. This was the same mistake made 5,000 years ago in Mesopotamia: deforestation there increased the erosion of saline mountain soils and salinized the arable land, thereby reducing food production and contributing to the empire's decline. The Greeks, Romans, and other southern Europeans learned similar lessons as they, too, deforested and eroded their lands, depleted their soils, and killed their wildlife. The same was true in ancient North Africa, China, and elsewhere.

The world's forests, which once covered 40 percent of the Earth, have been reduced by more than 30 percent since humans first began cutting them down thousands of years ago. The reality is even worse than these statistics indicate: only 12 percent of the Earth is still covered by *intact* forest ecosystems. More-over, the pace of global deforestation is extremely fast. Between 1950 and 1991, world consumption of wood for fuel and materials rose two-and-a-half times to 3.4 billion cubic meters. World paper consumption has grown about tenfold since 1930.

Rising demand for lumber and plywood has made tropical wood a disastrously profitable commodity. For this and other reasons, half of the world's tropical rain forests have been lost, just in the past fifty years. Central and South America, North America, Africa, and Asia have sustained major forest losses. Ecologically unique tropical forest ecosystems, such as those of Madagascar, the Philippines, and Hawaii, with many rare endemic species, have been plundered for their timber.

Rapid forest losses are not confined to the tropics. Today, chainsaws are consuming the great northern forests of Siberia at twice the annual rate of deforestation in the Brazilian Amazon. Old-growth forest logging has been particularly savage and unremitting in British Columbia and elsewhere in western Canada too. More than 50 percent of the old growth of coastal British Columbia has already been logged. Nineteen of the twenty primary watersheds on Vancouver Island have already been clearcut. (A primary watershed is one that opens directly to the sea.) Government logging plans target more than 90 percent of Canada's old growth for extinction. If history is a guide, Canadians may well repeat, albeit more rapidly, the mistakes the United States has made with its forests over the past four centuries.

One need not be an ecological purist to be profoundly concerned about forest losses. The gross environmental impacts from such losses range from the merely costly to the catastrophic. Deforestation over large land areas can produce drought, flooding, desertification, soil degradation, erosion, and thus siltation. In turn, siltation can cause severe damage to streams, rivers, wetlands, reservoirs, lakes, canals, dams, and harbors. The effects of deforestation also extend far beyond the cutover land to rivers, bays, and oceans. Salmon catches in rivers and oceans have declined steeply as spawning streams fill with debris and silt, depriving people, bears, eagles, and orcas of important food sources.

## U.S. Deforestation:
## How It Started and How It "Stopped"

U.S. forest cover was inexorably reduced by logging over centuries of European settlement. From the billion or so forested acres found in what is now the United States, including Alaska, a low point in forest area of 567 million acres was reached sometime about 1900. Since then, the area of land in forest has increased somewhat due to the reconversion of marginal agricultural land to forest. Comparing the original expanse of American forest land across what is now the "Lower 48" states to U.S. forest area in 1990 indicates that the United States now has 250 million to 310 million acres of forest less than in 1600, depending on which expert's estimate you accept. (Estimates vary for legitimate reasons, such as at what point a plantation of tree seedlings comprises a forest.)

Whereas forest cover losses stabilized nationwide around 1900, some regions continued to lose net forest cover until 1920 or later. Even today, certain regional forest types, such as California's oak woodlands, are declining in acreage. If one considers *native* forest rather than forest area per se, then forest losses in some regions are continuing to the present, since timber companies often reforest with different species (or different proportions of species) than a site originally had. Nationwide, however, U.S. forest acreage in 1992—737 million acres—was about the same as in 1920, although much of what passes for forest is a faint shadow of its former grandeur and, in many places, is scarcely better than a tree farm. Today's acreage represents a recovery in area of about 170 million acres over the nadir of forest acreage that occurred in 1900.

Forest removal began relatively slowly at first in what is now the United States, constrained by early settlers' small numbers and technological limitations. Thus it took settlers a full two-and-a-half centuries—from 1600 to 1850—to accomplish the first 40 percent of the total deforestation they eventually inflicted. But the rate of deforestation increased so quickly after 1850 that in the next 50 years, far more land—150 million acres—was deforested than in the previous 250 years.

Although U.S. wood growth in the aggregate now exceeds consumption, that statistic disguises the fact that, even while the total area in forest has been largely unchanged in the United States for decades, certain ecosystems have been more heavily depleted or damaged, while others have had an opportunity to recover. During the 1980s, for example, bottomland hardwood acreage in the South was converted to agricultural use so rapidly and extensively that, by 1985, only a million of the original 24 million acres of bottomland hardwoods remained in the lower Mississippi River Delta. Similarly hidden in the overall statistic, softwood cutting on commercial timber lands substantially exceeded growth from the late 1950s or early 1960s well into the 1980s.

And although temperate zone forests increased globally by about 5 million acres between 1980 and 1990, the aggregate estimates of timber acreage obscure localized regional devastation and qualitative changes in forest condition. In Europe, more than a fifth of the trees have moderate to severe defoliation, most probably caused by air pollution, drought, nutrient loss, and insect damage. Aggregate forest loss data also typically do not highlight the losses in old growth versus other forests.

Today, only about 1 percent of western European forests can still be considered old growth (greater than 200 years of age in this case and harboring "a natural range" of indigenous species).

The colonists who arrived in what is now the United States found a largely unspoiled natural environment with wild forest covering more than 1 billion acres, including Alaska. Much of the continent, however, was intensively managed with fire by the original Native American inhabitants. Their periodic fires, and those ignited by lightning, kept the Great Plains east of the Mississippi River in grasses and herbs, instead of allowing forest establishment. Native Americans also kept eastern forests of oak, elm, ash, and hickory open and healthy by burning them frequently. These early American forest stewards not only hunted and gathered in the forest and farmed in clearings, but also "outplanted" desirable plants to use for food, basketry, and other crafts. Forests were the Native American's gardens and orchards, as well as enormous storehouses of fish, fowl, and meat. As long as the forests were cared for and protected, their magnificent bounty was endless.

Before the colonial era, logging in North America meant that a Native American went into the woods, carefully selected a tree, and, after an appropriate ritual to propitiate its spirit, laboriously cut down the tree with a stone hatchet to build a dugout or removed its bark to sheathe a canoe. The sanctity of the natural world was not a belief unique to Native American culture. Certain groves, and even large parts of forests, have been regarded as sacred in Africa, Europe, India, and China since ancient times. Groves were sacred temples for the Druids, for example, and sanctuaries for the pantheistic ancient Athenians. The Chinese have preserved groves of sacred trees near temples since Confucian times, and before the British came to the Uttarahkand region of India, no one was allowed to harm the vegetation of Uttarahkand's sacred areas in any way. In their wisdom, religion and folk custom created early forest nature preserves in various cultures.

By contrast, early European settlers of New World appear to have been blind to the miraculous and sacred dimensions of forest life. They neither managed the forests sustainably nor valued them as ecological phenomena. They saw only game, lumber, and firewood to be taken and land to be cleared. Steeped in a Protestant work ethic and a utilitarian materialism, they viewed the wilderness as a hostile adversary to be tamed and replaced with the blessings of "civilization." The construction of their towns and cities, and the development of their industries, required a continual supply of timber and fuel. That meant incessant forest clearing, so the settlers industriously hacked and hewed the forest to build their villages, roads, ships, farms, and factories. From the days of earliest settlement until 1880, by far most of the wood cut was used for fuel, while the rest went for building materials or was cleared for the conversion of forest to farms.

Deforestation first began in the East, localized initially in coastal regions and around towns and cities. Anyone who could swing an ax took what he could, giving little or nothing back to the land. As those lands were cleared and settled, and the more accessible forests were converted to agricultural uses, the settlers pushed steadily west, leaving stumps and fields behind them. For a hundred years after the nation's founding, it was federal policy to dispose of public land freely or cheaply to homesteaders, miners, and grazers, to encourage settlement and promote economic development. Much of the nation's forests, ranges, and mineral wealth were thus put into a multitude of private hands.

At first, only a small percentage of the forests were cleared. After all, they stretched for hundreds of millions of acres. But eventually, as cities developed, huge areas were cleared. By the

1860s, a commercial timber industry had come into being, and the wood chips and sawdust really began to fly. Eager for abundant supplies of trees after the Civil War, the timber industry discovered the pine forests of Michigan, Minnesota, and Wisconsin and logged them as fast as it could, leaving only "stump lands." From the onset of logging in the Great Lakes region after the Civil War, it took only a few decades to remove three-quarters of the area's standing timber. Sold to homesteaders, the stump lands proved unsuitable for agriculture.

The new timber industry next moved south to log the pine forests that stretched from Virginia through Texas. By the 1920s, timber companies had reduced the forests there, too, and were off to the Pacific Northwest. Under the influence of abundant rainfall, the region's ancient Douglas fir, spruce, and hemlock grew two to three times as tall as the trees of the eastern hardwood forests. The giant trees were a lumberman's dream, but the legacy of destruction the industry had left behind across the country was beginning to catch up with it. An era of forest regulation was beginning. Some forest treasures were temporarily placed off-limits to the timber industry in parks and National Forests.

As noted, net losses of U.S. forest land ceased around 1900, and forest area increased slightly to 1920, at which point the amount of land in forest cover stabilized. This was caused by the gradual abandonment of farmland in the East and South, beginning in the 1880s, and by a tapering off in forest-to-farm conversions. Many of these abandoned farms naturally reverted to forest, and the forest-to-farm conversions largely ended in the 1930s. Thus U.S. forests increased by 40 million acres from 1920 to 1930. Net forest losses nationwide also stopped because of technological changes. Coal and oil replaced wood as fuel, and motorized vehicles replaced draft animals. Consequently, much less farmland was required for pasturing stock and raising forage. Improvements in agricultural technology also led to large increases in agricultural productivity, which meant less farmland was needed. Improvements in lumber mill efficiency also made it possible to get more usable wood from each tree as mills acquired smaller, more exact saws and, in the late twentieth century, obtained "smarter," automated cutting equipment.

To sum up, the trend toward progressive deforestation of the United States came to a halt through a combination of technological change and economic forces, albeit bolstered by conservation sentiment and forest conservation legislation (described in later chapters). Today, with about the same total amount of land area in forests as in 1920, we still convert about 500,000 acres of forest every year to farms and urban uses, but U.S. forest acreage is nonetheless on the increase, if one includes tree plantations that as yet contain only seedlings. In addition to tree plantations and reforestation efforts, many small marginal farms in the Northeast have been abandoned during the past fifty to a hundred years and have reverted from field to forest or brush. The percent of land in forests in the Northeast has therefore increased in many areas, reaching close to 60 percent for New York, Connecticut, and Pennsylvania.

In the 1930s, a cooperative forest fire control program launched by the U.S. Forest Service involving state agencies and private timber owners also began reducing forest losses. Its success alleviated timber growers' fears that their timber would be destroyed before it could be sold, and the program thus contributed to their willingness to risk retaining standing timber.

As recently as the 1940s, timber was still so cheap that it cost less to buy a stand and cut it than to plant an equivalent acreage in seedlings, not to mention raising them to commercial size. Only when lumber prices rose in the 1960s, in response to diminished supply, did reforestation begin to be widely practiced on commercial timber lands.

## The Price Forests Have Paid

Although some of our replacement forests are healthy, others show signs of neglect, mismanagement, and the ravages of diseases and pests of European origin, such as gypsy moth infestations and Dutch elm disease. Still others bear damage inflicted by multiple pollutants, especially ozone, and to a lesser extent acid rain. The affected trees may show a variety of symptoms: leaf loss, discoloration, and abnormalities; reduced growth, branch dieback, and increased susceptibility to illness and pests; and eventually premature death.

Whereas trees planted by timber companies and private landowners helped defray forest losses from lumbering, the second-, third-, and fourth-growth forests produced in the United States have tended to be vastly inferior in native biodiversity, volume, and size to the original old-growth forests that stood on the lands just eighty to a hundred years earlier. Much of the eastern and southern replacement forests today are simplified and crowded brushy stands of small, narrow-girth trees. Gone are the chestnuts and elms, victims of diseases from abroad. Some oaks and maples are now being attacked by fungi. Beech, dogwood, sycamore, white ash, balsam fir, and hemlock are threatened by disease and pests, too. Exotic plant species from Europe and Asia have also invaded and displaced native species, changing the forests in fundamental ways. High-grading— culling the best trees by selective cutting—has removed many of the finest seed trees from the woods. In addition, the new woodlands are often fragmented in small, disconnected lots, with a high ratio of edge to interior. This changes the habitat and reduces the niches suitable for deep-forest songbirds and other forest species. Simultaneously and tragically, many migratory songbirds are losing their Southern Hemisphere habitat to deforestation.

Even though today's second- and third-growth forests are not the equals of earlier old growth, many wildlife species can thrive in these forests and have rebounded from low population levels at the turn of the century. Populations of beaver, elk, pronghorn antelope, wild turkey, and white-tailed deer have all boomed as hunting has been regulated more scientifically, based on game population surveys, and forest habitats have increased and been protected in national and state wildlife refuges and on well-managed private lands. Unfortunately, other, nongame species, such as the red-cockaded woodpecker, have not thrived, and still others have gone extinct.

Forest protection in the future thus needs to involve more than just continued vigilance to safeguard old growth from logging, and more than just holistic, sustained-yield forestry to maintain the health of productive timber lands. It must also include restoring populations of sensitive, threatened, and endangered species and the nursing of deteriorating forests, old and new, back to health by controlling incursions of invasive species that threaten to overrun native ecosystems, even in protected national parks and wilderness. Chapters 10, 11, and 13 discuss how to accomplish some of these goals.

## Public Lands

Of the 737 million forested acres in the United States in 1990, two-thirds—or 483 million acres—were productive timber lands; the remainder were unproductive or off-limits to logging because of park, wilderness, or protected watershed designations. Who owns and controls U.S. forests? Although our National Forests are 191.6 million acres in size, they contain only 85 million acres of commercial forest land—18 percent of the country's total. Another 11 percent of U.S. commercial forests are in other federal, state, county, and municipal ownership. Thus the public owns and in theory manages nearly 30 percent of the nation's commercially productive forest land.

Timber companies own a surprisingly small portion of the nation's commercial timber lands—only 15 percent. Roughly 56 percent of commercial forest remains in private hands. Despite the small share of total forest land that is in commercial timber, these lands produced about a third of the nation's timber harvest —more than twice the output of the National Forests. This is largely because industry in the West managed to acquire the nation's most productive timber lands before the National Forests were established.

Wood imports currently supply an important part of our domestic timber consumption. In 1985 the nation consumed about 18 billion cubic feet of wood cut annually from roughly 5 million acres of forest. About 5.2 billion cubic feet of that wood were imported, most of it from Canada; exports were about 1.5 billion cubic feet. Domestic wood growth—more than 22 billion cubic feet per year—currently exceeds total domestic consumption by a significant amount, even without imports, so no commercial timber shortage is foreseen, especially since standing timber volumes in 1990 were 25 percent greater than in 1950. Therefore, forest protectors can take heart: forest conservation and protection (see Chapter 13) will not bring about any timber famine. Quite the contrary, wise stewardship will preserve, enhance, and perpetuate our forest resources.

# CHAPTER 4

# CONSERVATION EFFORTS

> How would you feel if you knew that the oldest living
> beings on earth had all been converted into money and
> you would never again see them, and your children
> would never have a chance to see them?
>
> Chris Maser, *Sustainable Forestry*

 Starting in the mid-1860s, early conservationists
such as George Perkins Marsh, who witnessed
widespread forest destruction, were becoming
alarmed about the possibility of future national
timber shortages. More than 300 years of deforestation had already
taken place in the United States. At last, a few farsighted
and public-spirited citizens, scientists, naturalists, and sportsmen
were starting the slow process of convincing the government
that the fate of the nation's forests was cause for concern. They
aroused the scientific and media communities and eventually
brought their fears of future timber famines to the Congress and
state legislatures. Initially, those bodies took little effective action. Private citizens outside government, however, took responsiblity for waking up their elected representatives and making a case for conservation.

At first, few conservationists defended the forests for their intrinsic value. One exception was the passionate and enlightened
conservationist-explorer-scientist John Muir. As a boy, Muir had
helped his family clear wild forests in Wisconsin so that the fam-

ily could farm. But as a man, speaking from personal knowledge gained in long, solitary journeys on foot through the forests of the United States and Canada, Muir urged the protection of forests for their beauty, wildlife, and natural power to heal and uplift the human spirit. By the 1870s, Muir and conservationists such as forester Dr. Franklin B. Hough were calling insistently for federal action.

Several states also awakened to the need for forest conservation in the 1860s and 1870s, but usually became active only after timber companies had already ravaged their lands. State forest protection efforts were generally limited to establishing commissions of inquiry to document the extent of forest destruction or to creating weak state forestry associations, few of which had trained staff or adequate financial resources. These early ineffectual efforts bear a curious resemblance to contemporary efforts by multinational organizations to protect tropical forests (see Chapter 12).

Early conservationists shared some of the Progressive movement's concerns about monopolies. By advocating government control of forests, conservationists sought to protect the public domain from the thrall of the timber magnates and robber barons who had seized control of other extractive industries and were adept at consolidating in their own hands resources that had initially been intended by law for the benefit of the many.

Congress first responded to pressure for forest conservation in 1872 by creating Yellowstone Park in Wyoming and then by passing the ill-fated Timber Culture Act of 1873 to encourage homesteaders to protect trees. The act led to widespread land fraud, however, and upon repeal, was replaced by the Forest Reserve Act of 1891. The Forest Reserve Act marks a transition in public land policy "from disposal to retention" of the public domain. The act authorized the president to set aside (reserve) millions of acres of land from "public entry," which meant sale to the public, in order to protect watersheds and establish parks. President Benjamin Harrison used his new authority promptly to designate reserves, and by 1897, during Grover Cleveland's term, 40 million acres had been set aside.

Bernard Fernow, an émigré German forester who headed the U.S. Bureau of Forestry, urged Congress as early as 1891 to manage the new forest reserves for a continuous (sustained) yield of timber. He was the principal author of the Forest Management Act, known as the Organic Act of 1897. This act established the purposes of the forest reserves: they were to protect watersheds and provide a timber supply for the nation. The act also established management principles for the reserves. Fernow had the foresight to recognize as early as 1902, in his work *Economics of Forestry*, that timber companies did not, and would not for the foreseeable future, have sufficient economic incentives to manage their timber on a sustainable yield basis. He therefore advocated government control of forests.

The federal forest reserves were transferred from the Department of the Interior to the Department of Agriculture's Bureau of Forestry in 1905 after a long campaign by then–bureau head Gifford Pinchot, an intimate friend of President Theodore Roosevelt and an early protégé of Muir. The reserves became the core of the nation's National Forests. In 1907, the reserves were renamed the National Forests; and the Bureau of Forestry was renamed the U.S. Forest Service.

As outlined by Chief Forester Pinchot, the National Forests were to be put to prompt and businesslike *use*, albeit a conservative use, which preserved their permanent value. Pinchot's goal was to ensure the continued prosperity of the nation's agricultural, lumbering, mining, and livestock interests through an ample supply of timber. The forests, he said, were to be used "for the permanent good of the whole people and not for the benefit of individuals and companies." He also decreed that "where conflicting interests must be reconciled[,] the question will always be decided from the standpoint of the greatest good of the greatest number in the long run" (see *Forest and Range Policy,* by Samuel Dana Trask and Sally K. Fairfax). More concerned with using the National Forests than with their protection, however, Pinchot opened the National Forests to livestock grazing. He also successfully opposed establishment of wildlife preserves in the forests and betrayed the trust of John Muir by siding with those who, over Muir's fervent opposition, were to build Hetch Hetchy Dam in Yosemite, the first dam to be sited in a national park.

By 1907, Roosevelt, under Pinchot and Muir's influence, had exercised the authority granted him by the Forest Reserve Act to set aside 100 million additional acres as National Forests, mostly in the West. The Weeks Act of 1911 extended the forest reserves to the East, where most of the timber had already been cut. The act was passed to accomplish flood and fire control and watershed protection, as well as out of a desire to secure recreational opportunities on public lands.

As the federal government began protecting forest reserves in the late nineteenth century, a parallel nongovernmental conservation movement was launched and sustained by the amateur efforts of private citizens, generally men of wealth and position. George Bird Grinnell, a hunter-conservationist appalled by the slaughter of birds for the plume trade founded the National Audubon Society in 1886. Although the protection of birds was its initial mission, that concern led the Society to work for the protection of diverse bird habitats, including forests. In time the Society's agenda broadened, and by the late twentieth century the organization had a following of 570,000 members.

Another private organization that helped form early forest policy was the Boone and Crockett Club, a small but influential hunting club of conservation-minded sportsmen founded in 1887 by Theodore Roosevelt and a number of fellow big game hunters, including Grinnell. The membership eventually included Forest Service chief Gifford Pinchot and renowned wildlife ecologist Aldo Leopold, foremost exponent of the seminal land ethic concept, which asserted an ethical obligation of land stewardship. While promoting rifle hunting, the Boone and Crockett Club lobbied for the enactment of the first game laws, such as those protecting migratory birds, and for the establishment of national forests, wildlife refuges, and national parks.

The power of the inspired and committed citizen working on behalf of nature is splendidly epitomized in the accomplishments of John Muir. Working independently as a writer and public speaker, Muir collaborated with his publisher, Robert Underwood Johnson, the editor of *Century* magazine, to campaign relentlessly for forest protection. In 1889, *Century* issued a call for protection of all forests on federal land and for a national forest plan. Muir's lyrical nature writing and advocacy coupled with Johnson's publishing and lobbying launched a successful campaign for the eventual creation of Yosemite National Park in 1890. Some of the land was already under the state of California's ineffectual guardianship. Muir helped draw new boundaries to protect 1,500 square miles of unparalleled beauty surrounding Yosemite Valley in the heart of the park.

In 1892, Muir and twenty-seven other Californians founded the Sierra Club. It was part alpine club and part conservation organization and was modeled after the Appalachian Mountain Club. One of the group's guiding precepts was Muir's firm belief that bringing people into the wilderness would create converts for conservation. This conviction provided the impetus for the Club's wilderness and mountaineering outings, Sierra Nevada trail building, and educational programs. The Club, however, was not just dedicated to promoting the exploration and enjoyment of mountains. Club leaders wanted to protect the forests and other natural features of the Sierra.

In the Club's early years, Muir worked closely with Johnson and with Harvard botanist Charles Sprague Sargent, a pioneer of the forest conservation movement. Sargent had conducted a survey of the nation's forests in 1880 and for years thereafter had advocated creation of a federal forestry commission to survey western forests. Finally authorized in 1894, the western survey, on which Sargent also labored, provided the justification that President Grover Cleveland needed in 1897 to set aside by administrative action more than 21 million acres of public land as forest reserves.

With the fame that Muir's writings and successes in protecting Yosemite brought, Muir, Johnson, and Sargent used their influence to lobby Interior secretaries and other powerful government officials for forest protection. In 1903, President Theodore Roosevelt invited Muir to camp with him in Yosemite, and Muir's eloquence and passion in defense of nature made an enormous impression on Roosevelt, beautifully chronicled in *John Muir and His Legacy*, by Stephen Fox. Following their trip, Roosevelt had the Sierra Nevada forest reserve extended as far north as Mount Shasta. During his presidency, Roosevelt created or enlarged thirty-two forest reserves totaling 75 million acres, in addition to numerous wildlife reserves, parks, and national monuments.

Through the involvement of Sierra Club members in outdoor activities, the Club became inexorably drawn more and more deeply into protecting forests and other natural resources. To date, the Club has fought many successful battles for the establishment and enlargement of national parks, national forests, national monuments, wilderness areas, and wildlife refuges, and against the establishment of major dams in parks and other scenic areas. By the 1950s, the Club was broadening its outdoor activities and areas of concern beyond California to other states. Gradually, as the conservation movement of the 1950s and 1960s metamorphosed into the environmental movement of the later twentieth century, the Club became a "full service" environmental organization engaged in virtually every type of environmental issue, from protection of forests, deserts, prairies, air, soil, and water to energy, agricultural, toxics, and trade policies. Today, the Club has more than 600,000 members in 57 chapters and 370 groups.

Other national and regional conservation organizations have also played pivotal roles in the protection of forests and other natural resources using a variety of techniques. The Wilderness Society, founded in 1935 by forester and plant pathologist Robert Marshall and others, was dedicated to "fighting off invasion of the wilderness" and promoting an appreciation of its values. The Society battled on the legislative front as well as in the courts for wilderness protection and for proper management of the National Forests. In the late 1940s, Wilderness Society director Howard Zahniser reintroduced the idea of a national wilderness protection system and began campaigning for it. (The idea was first articulated in 1921 by regional planner Benton MacKaye, father of the Appalachian Trail.) After years of effort, Zahniser's campaign and early legislative drafting culminated in the passage of the 1964 Wilderness Act. The act established the National Wilderness Preservation System and protected more than 9 million acres of wilderness. By 1997, the system included more than 104 million acres, including more than 50 million acres in Alaska.

Still other private conservation organizations, such as The Nature Conservancy and The Trust for Public Land, concentrated on the acquisition of ecologically important and threatened lands, especially those critical to preservation of endangered species and biodiversity. The National Wildlife Federation and Defenders of Wildlife stressed the protection of wildlife and related issues. To a large extent, the robust nongovernmental conservation movement was necessitated by the frequent widespread failures of governmental agencies to prevent the deterioration of native ecosystems and to protect wildlife.

As early as 1897, the Organic Act had codified into law the idea that the national forests (then known as forest reserves) were not to be managed exclusively for any one industry or to yield a single product, but for a variety of benefits. This multiple-use principle was later elaborated in the Multiple-Use Sustained-Yield Act of 1960. The 1960 act's multiple-use doctrine requires that the renewable resources in the National Forests be managed in a balanced and coordinated way so that no one use excludes the others and so that the productivity of the land remains unimpaired. The U.S. Forest Service supported the act's passage in the hope that it would preclude the large-scale designation of forest lands as wilderness, a single use that would have precluded logging. (The act does, however, require the Forest Service to recognize wilderness preservation as a legitimate use among other forest land uses.) The sustained-yield provisions of the Multiple-Use Sustained-Yield Act prescribe that the National Forests must be managed so as to make possible a nondeclining rate of timber production in perpetuity. Other activities in the forest, such as mining, grazing, recreation (including wilderness enjoyment), and hunting, were also recognized by the act as uses to be sustained through prudent long-term management.

Unfortunately, as discussed in Chapter 5, the multiple-use doctrine was more often honored in the breach than the observance. The term multiple-use can be used to mask extremely damaging forest practices. For most of the post-World War II period, timber extraction has been the dominant use of the National Forests to which other uses have had to yield. The Forest Service has received timber production quotas from Congress that have often resulted in logging rates far in excess of what can be sustained. A veritable tug of war typically takes place between Congress, the administration, and the Forest Service over how much of the Forest Service's roadless areas ought to be preserved as wilderness and how much ought to be logged. (Congress, the environmental community, timber interests, and the Forest Service also spar over timber production quotas.) All parties to these contests are spurred by conflicting pressures from pro-wilderness environmental forces and anti-wilderness timber industry interests. In 1976, during the administration of President Jimmy Carter, the Forest Service formally addressed the question of how much wilderness to save from the chainsaw in its first Roadless Area Review and Evaluation (RARE I), which inventoried roadless areas and made recommendations for their management. RARE I proposed that only 12 million of the the Forest Service's 56 million roadless acres should be protected as wilderness. After a legal challenge from environmentalists, the RARE I study was invalidated in federal court for failing to adequately assess the plan's environmental impacts.

In 1978, a second Forest Service plan, known as RARE II, proposed wilderness protection for 16 million acres but also increased the acreage designated for possibly destructive multiple uses. RARE II became mired in additional litigation and eventually was found to be in violation of the National Environmental Policy Act for failing to adequately consider wilderness as a use for some of the roadless lands. Thus RARE II also was never implemented. The Carter administration came to a close without bequeathing a formal wilderness protection plan for the nation's roadless National Forest areas. President Carter did, however, sign the Alaska National Interest Lands Conservation Act of 1980, which gave federal protection to millions of acres of forested (and other) wilderness lands, and the Alaska Native Claims Settlement Act, which ceded millions of acres more to the control of corporations established by Native Alaskan peoples.

Despite the absence of a comprehensive successor to RARE II for determining the fate of roadless areas, for the past two decades Congress has sporadically added wilderness to the National Wilderness Preservation System while opening roadless areas to development, all on an ad hoc basis, responding expediently to a host of political pressures, including those emanating from the White House. The Reagan and Bush administrations that followed President Carter were largely hostile or indifferent to additional wilderness designations, although dozens of wilderness bills passed Congress despite lack of administration support. The Clinton administration, by contrast, has been much more supportive of wilderness establishment. Today, however, millions of acres of land still remain roadless, their fate undetermined and controversial as ever.

The National Forest Management Act of 1976 (NFMA) was ostensibly passed to provide more specific direction to the Forest Service in managing the forests, consistent with the mandates of the Multiple-Use Sustained-Yield Act. The NFMA indeed does reaffirm the principles of multiple use and sustained yield. However, because the Forest Service was very much in the thrall of the timber industry and its congressional allies during the postwar period, the NFMA in practice—implemented by friends of the timber industry—allowed the Forest Service to abandon sustained-yield selective management and to permit clearcutting, by creating broad exceptions to the Multiple-Use Sustained-Yield Act. The NFMA, however, and contemporaneous legislation—the Federal Land Policy and Management Act of 1976 (FLPMA) and the Forest and Rangeland Renewable Resources Planning Act of 1974 (RPA)—stress the use of resource inventories for forest and range planning and management. These conservation laws decrease the chances that nontimber values will simply be accidentally overlooked and increase the chances for systematic resource management.

Among its positive features, the NFMA requires the Forest Service to prepare an interdisciplinary forest plan for managing each National Forest and stipulates that a reforestation plan must be included in every National Forest timber sale so that cutover lands can be restocked "with assurance" within five years of the final harvest. The NFMA prohibits logging "where soil, slope, or other watershed conditions" will be "irreversibly damaged" and requires each sale to include a "sale area improvement plan" that often outlines mitigation measures required to counter logging impacts. Under the act, forest planning is to be comprehensive and integrated for multiple uses, not exclusively for harvesting timber. Logging rates are not to exceed sustainable limits. Nevertheless, laxity in interpretation and enforcement has been a problem: flagrantly unsustainable timber exploitation has continued under the act's aegis, even though the importance of other nontimber uses, such as recreation, watershed, fish and wildlife, was formally recognized and accorded more attention. Chapter 5 reviews new Forest Service policies and indications that the Forest Service intends to dramatically alter past policies that often condoned forest degradation on a grand scale.

# THE U.S. FOREST SERVICE

> The forest is not a factory for goods and services. It is a
> living entity which we have an ethical obligation to re-
> spect and perpetuate, even the parts which seemingly
> have no present use to human beings.
>
> Tim Foss, "New Forestry: A State of Mind,"
> in *Restoration Forestry*

The agitation for conservation that began in the
1860s did eventually produce important results.
These came in the form of protective national forest legislation, and the establishment of more than
190 million acres of National Forests along with the U.S. Forest
Service to oversee them, as well as the designation of tens of
millions of acres of wilderness and thousands of miles of wild
and scenic river corridor. Other federal agencies were entrusted
with stewardship of millions of additional acres of national
parks, monuments, wildlife refuges, and protected grasslands, all
sequestered from development to varying degrees. These federal
resources are augmented by a multitude of state forests, parks,
and refuges. The management of public forests by their official
stewards, however, is usually far from what good forestry dictates or what the American people have a right to expect.

The case of the 17-million-acre Tongass National Forest is
an instructive example. Largest of all our National Forests, the

Tongass National Forest in Southeast Alaska is the largest old-growth temperate rain forest left in the United States. This majestic greenbelt stretches south of Ketchikan across the Alaska Panhandle, from the islands and misty fjords of the Gulf of Alaska to the state's interior border with British Columbia. Logging was originally sanctioned and encouraged here by the federal government, which, through the Forest Service, gave two large timber companies—the Ketchikan Pulp Company and the Alaska Pulp Company—fifty-year logging concessions at bargain basement prices. The companies "paid less than the price of a cheeseburger for a 500-year-old tree," according to Timothy Egan in a September 1995 article in the *New York Times*. They took advantage of their concessions to clearcut forest lands and export the logs and pulp to Japan, South Korea, and Taiwan. In the process, the companies did enormous damage to the forest, and the Ketchikan Pulp Company, owned by Louisiana-Pacific, left a potent legacy of toxic pollution on the coast of Southeast Alaska in the sediments of Ketchikan's Ward Cove, where it dumped its poisonous pulp-mill effluent in violation of state and federal permits. The casualties of the Tongass clearcutting include silted salmon streams where world-class king salmon spawn, and once-forested but now-denuded crags where wolverines, gray wolves, and grizzlies recently roamed. Whereas the Tongass timber cannot be profitably cut on a large commercial scale today in an ecologically sustainable manner, fishing and tourism industries in the area can provide more jobs and revenue indefinitely than can continued destruction of the old-growth forest. (This is not to suggest that the forest might not support a small-scale local timber industry on a sustainable basis.)

The Japanese-owned Alaska Pulp Company abandoned its operations in the Tongass in 1993. The Forest Service subsequently canceled the company's fifty-year timber concession, which had given Alaska Pulp permission to cut 2 billion board feet of Tongass timber by 2011. The Ketchikan Pulp Company left the Tongass after pleading guilty to violating federal water pollution laws with discharges from its Ketchikan mill, which ground logs into pulp for export. In 1996 the company announced it would have to abandon its Tongass operations because Forest Service regulations would make further work there unprofitable. The company's opponents said it was unwilling to make the investments needed to correct its water pollution violations.

In a classic case of pandering to special interests at the expense of the nation and the environment, Alaska's two senators, Frank Murkowski and Ted Stevens, tried to obtain federal subsidies to continue the Tongass logging, but could not persuade the 104th Congress to go along. From the standpoint of the public treasury, the decision came not a moment too soon. Timber sales in the Tongass cost taxpayers more than $102 million to facilitate clearcutting by logging companies, just from 1992 through 1994, according to the U.S. General Accounting Office.

## Demand for Federal Timber Accelerates

National forests have not always been managed as they were in the Tongass. At one time, trees were selectively logged at a moderate pace rather than clearcut, and it seemed as if the National Forests might be treated as a public trust. In the first decades after the U.S. Forest Service was established in 1907, commercial timber companies did not want timber to be sold from the National Forests, since the federal timber would compete with sales of their privately owned timber holdings. As late as World War II, only 2 percent of the nation's timber came from the National Forests. But by about 1950, a turnabout occurred. Much privately owned timber had been cut during the war, and a shortage of private timber had developed by the war's end. The scarcity of private timber became acute enough to arouse the commercial lumber companies' interest in the National Forests.

Until this point, the Forest Service had mainly practiced multiple-use and sustained-yield management during the first half of the twentieth century. The Forest Service thereupon shifted toward industrial forest management. This meant clearcutting at the expense of long-term forest sustainability, aggressive road building, intensified logging, and managment of the National Forests for timber as the dominant forest use, rather than for multiple uses.

Whereas only 1.5 billion board feet per year of timber had been cut in National Forests in the early 1940s, and whereas the cut was still only 3.5 billion board feet in 1950, the timber industry and Congress began pressuring the Forest Service to steeply increase its harvest rate. In response, the Forest Service abandoned its previous insistence on selective logging under sustained-yield guidelines and began to allow wholesale clearcutting. This ended the era of forest custodianship and marked the beginning of aggressive resource exploitation of the National Forests. As larger mandatory timber harvest allowances were imposed and as more timber sales were ordered, the rules for timber appraisals and sales were made progressively less protective of the forest, and clearcutting increased. By 1970, timber industry pressure on the Forest Service had increased to the point that 13.6 billion board feet were being taken annually from National Forests—almost four times the 1950 level. The logging rate remained at about 13 billion board feet—which the Forest Service contended was still a sustainable level—through 1990.

## Below-Cost Timber Sales

During most of the half-century-long post–World War II period of aggressively expanded timber cutting, the Forest Service accepted even very low offers for its commercial timber. Forest Service costs for managing timber sales and expediting timber removal for logging companies frequently far exceeded the government's proceeds from the sale. As a result, public timber was often sold at an outright loss, and valuable opportunities for multiple use were simultaneously foreclosed, even though non-extractive uses—such as recreation, fish, and wildlife—still exceed the value of timber, grazing, and mining in eight of nine Forest Service regions.

Thus, not only have National Forests suffered from federally sanctioned logging, but at Congress's direction, the public has been forced to subsidize the damage. The Wilderness Society estimated that such below-cost sales cost the public $21 billion dollars between 1975 and 1985 alone. Timber-sale spending by the Forest Service was mainly for road construction required for timber harvests and for management and administrative expenses. Private timber owners were also penalized: undervalued public timber dumped on the market through government subsidization artificially depressed timber prices and reduced the value of private holdings. How much wiser it would have been instead to have allowed the trees to grow and generally increase in value while applying the taxpayers' money to restoration and management of degraded forest lands, of which the Forest Service had ample supplies.

## Forest Service Problems and Remedies

Critics of the Forest Service believe that its foresters, who have on-the-ground responsibility for supervising timber sales, lack the professional prestige and administrative power to protect the forests from political appointees in the Forest Service bureaucracy who are too responsive to a Congress beholden to the timber industry.

Real opportunities for leadership have indeed been scarce in the Forest Service for much of the postwar period. Political and bureaucratic considerations have discouraged officials from real forest conservation and have absolved them of responsibility for mismanagement. Management authority has been diffused along an internal chain of command and outside of the service to contractors who perform much of the necessary field work. Also, by administrative design, federal foresters have been intentionally relocated every two to four years by the Forest Service to discourage "entrapment" by the local community, be it pro- or anti-logging. Foresters thus tend not to develop deep roots in communities near the forests they manage.

Whereas some of these practices can be altered by better leadership, some of the weaknesses in the Forest Service are only likely to be remedied when the economic interests of those controlling the forests are aligned with the public's long-term interest in forest welfare. This could happen if far-reaching political campaign reform occurred nationwide to reduce undue corporate influence on Congress. It could also happen if Forest Service employees' compensation were tied to increases in "forest capital," as reflected by improvements in forest health, structure, and quality, as well as by increases in the volume of standing timber.

In reaction to widely perceived violations of the public trust by the Forest Service and to increasing development pressure on the nation's remaining wild lands, Congress responded to insistent environmental lobbying by passing the Wilderness Act of 1964. The act set aside public lands securely beyond timber industry saws and other exploitative uses. In the same year, however, Congress also passed the National Forest Roads and Trails Systems Act, which put the Forest Service in the business of building logging roads for the timber industry to reduce costs to the logging companies. Over the years, the Forest Service has built 350,000 miles of permanent roads and uncounted miles of "temporary" roads in our National Forests. The length of the permanent roads alone is fourteen times the circumference of the Earth and eight times the federal highway system. These roads have taken millions of acres of forest out of timber and wildlife production. Worse, they have destroyed the wilderness character of millions of additional acres. The Forest Service estimated in 1985 that the roads it planned to build by 1995 would sacrifice 20 million acres of forest to road surface. And much road construction has been in areas that otherwise would have been candidates for wilderness designation and permanent protection. The Forest Service has often hastened to push roads into these areas precisely to foreclose their eligibility for wilderness protection. Fortunately, road construction rates in National Forests have decreased each year from 1990 through 1994. And while the Forest Service built 500 miles of new roads in 1994, it also returned about 2,000 miles of unneeded existing road to forest that year.

Other signs of hope are in evidence. In contrast to earlier cuts of 13 billion board feet per year, in 1995 the Forest Service allowed the cutting of under 5 billion board feet in the National Forests and offered 3.4 billion board feet for sale while reforesting about 440,000 acres of land in the same period. It also conducted silvicultural examinations on more than 2 million acres of forest. These exams were then used to prepare management prescriptions and conduct "timber stand improvement" work on more than a quarter of a million acres. The Forest Service is also trying to prevent and suppress insects, such as the gypsy moth, using an integrated pest management approach and is combating tree diseases that threaten standing timber.

## Reforestation of Public Lands

The quality of the reforestation and mitigation work done by commercial contractors on public lands depends on the standards to which the Forest Service is willing and able to hold its contractors, and on the dedication of the timber companies, which often operate under lax federal supervision. It also depends on the adequacy of the money bid in the timber sale to cover all concurrent reforestation work. In years when timber bids are low due to an economic recession and low timber demand, for example, funds may not be adequate for reforestation. The Forest Service must then seek the additional money from Congress, which may or may not appropriate it. If money does not arrive in a timely way, brush has more time to get established, which tends to increase eventual reforestation costs, since the larger the brush gets, the harder it is to control.

The Forest Service is also responsible for reforestation on previously cut but unrestored lands in the National Forests. This backlog work, too, depends on the availability of adequate funds, which must be appropriated by Congress and are subject to political considerations. Moreover, the Forest Service tends to be relatively uninterested in the reforestation of "low productivity" forest sites—those where timber production is under 50 cubic feet per acre per year—since these sites are unlikely to produce enough revenue to cover the cost of their repair. Economic considerations thus take precedence over potential ecological concerns.

Even when a commitment is made to reforest, reforestation efforts may fail for any number of reasons, ranging from inadequate site preparation, management, and/or planting personnel to failure to protect the seedlings from animals, drought, or frost. Sites are typically subject to one- and three-year postlogging survival exams, which mainly ensure that the trees are still alive. Systematic long-term ecological evaluation of reforestation efforts and their effects on watersheds and regional ecosystems are rarely if ever conducted. The Knutson-Vandenberg Act of 1930 gives the Forest Service the right to require deposits from timber companies to assure proper reforestation. In practice, however, the amount of the deposits may not be adequate to remedy problems arising from extraordinary events, such as droughts, fires, and insect invasions. The act generally provides only minimum funding necessary for reforestation and does not have to cover the costs of necessary follow-up "stand-tending activities." Furthermore, the Forest Service often applies the Knutson-Vandenberg monies for activities having nothing to do with the act's intended purposes, such as for road building. However, in contrast to conditions in 1900, when virtually no reforestation or long-term forest management was practiced, tree planting now occurs on millions of acres every year. A backlog of 80 million unstocked or poorly stocked acres of forest has been reforested since 1900.

## The Forest Service's Multiple Responsibilities

Due to its multiple-use mandate, many of the Forest Service's activities are not directly related to timber production. Today, for example, it not only manages 156 National Forests, but also administers 20 national grasslands and 71 experimental forests that belong to the National Forest System. The forests include 35 million acres of designated wilderness, almost 4,400 miles of National Wild and Scenic Rivers, and 379,000 miles of Forest Service roads. The Forest Service also runs some 18,000 recreational facilities and engages in scientific research at a network of forest experiment stations and wilderness research institutes.

The Forest Service is also required to manage fish, plants, wildlife, and habitat for sensitive, threatened, and endangered species. Along with other agencies, it is involved with projects such as grizzly bear recovery, gray wolf reintroductions, and restoration of the California condor and black-footed ferret. On its rangelands, it conducts some riparian area restoration, range improvement, and watershed protection, all from an ecosystem management perspective (a relatively new practice for the Forest Service). The agency also provides technical and financial assistance to nonindustrial state and private timber land owners. In addition, it fights forest fires; performs emergency watershed improvement work to combat erosion; conducts forest conservation education programs; and gathers scientific data on soil, water, air, and weather.

## The Forest Service Vows to Reinvent Itself

The Forest Service's scientific research encompasses the forest environment, forest protection, forest resource analysis, forest management research, forest products and harvesting, and ecosystem management, including large-scale ecosystem studies. The ecosystem management research is being conducted at a landscape level in an effort to learn how to manage natural resources in an integrated manner, rather than piece by piece. This landscape-level research includes efforts to identify ecosystems threatened by climate change and to model their probable response. From 1994 to 1996, for example, a study of alternative sustainable management scenarios for the entire Sierra Nevada ecosystem was prepared. Ironically, despite considerable domestic forest mismanagement, the Forest Service is increasingly active in exchanging scientific and technical information internationally to assist other nations in managing their forests and ranges to minimize damage to global ecosystems.

The agency currently reports that it is "redoubling efforts to ensure that all commodity production on USFS lands is done in an environmentally acceptable manner. Where commodity production cannot be achieved in such a manner, commodity outputs are being adjusted downwards." Consistent with these policy announcements, the Forest Service has been reducing reliance on clearcutting as a standard timber harvest method. Since 1991, the acreage clearcut has declined by about 25 percent to 100,000 acres.

Under its draft renewable resources program plan for 1995 (prepared decennially under provisions of the Forest and Rangeland Renewable Resources Planning Act of 1974 [RPA], as amended), the Forest Service has undertaken the challenging mission of fundamentally reinventing itself at the behest of President Clinton, who has directed the agency to "achieve sustainable forest management by the year 2000." To that end, the agency's long-term strategic plan outlines a set of laudable goals. Ecosystem protection and ecosystem management are to be cornerstones of national forest policy for at least the next decade. The restoration of ecosystems, too, will be a major goal in the years ahead. Another principal goal set forth is to provide multiple benefits for people *within the capabilities of ecosystems*— that is, consistent with maintenance of ecosystem health and diversity. Among specific priority actions, the Forest Service proposes to establish old-growth forest management areas and riparian conservation areas and to obliterate thousands of miles of Forest Service roads each year until the year 2000. "Maintaining or restoring conditions of late-successional and old-growth forest ecosystems will be the primary objective of old-growth management areas," the plan states. Declining timber harvests are projected along with a reduction in clearcutting from 18 percent to 4 percent of total acres cut.

The Forest Service also intends to increase its own accountability, expand its research and evaluation efforts, increase the use of prescribed fire as a management tool, augment efforts to enroll private forest landowners in its forest stewardship programs, and curtail resource extraction where necessary to protect ecosystems. All this, of course, is encouraging news, and friends of the forest will be watching eagerly in hopes that the laudable goals are matched by effective implementation and avoidance of further abusive forest practices.

## Public Participation in
## Forest Management and Planning

Under the Forest and Rangeland Renewable Resources Planning Act of 1974 (RPA) and amendments to it in the National Forest Management Act of 1976 (NFMA), opportunities have been provided for public participation in forest management plans and proposed timber sales in the National Forests.

National Forest plans are made and updated every ten or fifteen years. They not only determine which areas are destined for particular uses, such as logging, grazing, mining, watersheds, wildlife and fisheries, wilderness, research, or outdoor recreation, but also how those activities shall be managed. In addition to these National Forest rules, some states, such as California, have legislation that requires the state's Board of Forestry to solicit and consider public comment on proposed timber harvest plans.

Nationally, the RPA requires the Forest Service to prepare an assessment of renewable resources every ten years and to formulate a national renewable resource management policy along with multiple-use goals for the National Forests (and other public lands) in keeping with the Multiple-Use Sustained-Yield Act of 1960. The NFMA regulations and the Multiple-Use Sustained-Yield Act itself make three important stipulations: (1) management goals and objectives must protect and, where appropriate, enhance the quality of all renewable resources; (2) all forest uses must receive full and equal consideration; and (3) uses of the forest's renewable resources shall not diminish the land's future productivity. The Forest Service's legal commitment to sustainable resource management was significantly diluted, however, by the caveat in the NFMA regulations' definition of multiple use, that renewable resources are to be "utilized in a combination *that will best meet the needs of the American people; making the most judicious use of the land . . .*" (emphasis added) and by other allowable departures from sustained-yield timber management. The RPA provides the policy framework and goals within which national timber output goals must be set, consistent with the local resource capabilities of individual National Forests and other public lands. Forest activists and concerned citizens alike can provide detailed critical input to Forest Service management plans to help ensure that these significant commitments are fulfilled.

Forest planning is a particularly salient issue today as a major new round of National Forest plan revisions has already begun and will continue for the next several years in phases across different regions of the country. The first phase began in the central Rockies in 1996. Forest plans in the Southeast and in some northeastern forests will be reviewed in 1997 and 1998. Between 1997 and 2000, many other forest plans will be revised in the northern Rockies.

Despite the importance of these proceedings, many environmentalists are ambivalent about participating in them because of doubts about how effective their participation will be. The environmental community and the Forest Service have had an adversarial relationship for many years now. In 1996 the Sierra Club adopted a national policy opposing all commercial logging on the nation's federally owned public lands in reaction to persistent abuse of the National Forests (see Chapter 13). Other environmentalists have also become disillusioned and frustrated in attempting to influence the Forest Service planning process. To these activists, the process is a time-consuming sham designed to cloak predetermined industrial forestry policies in legitimacy. Nonetheless, forest activists generally still believe it is important to participate in the federal process and in state and local proceedings. They find that many state and local timber harvest plans can be improved, that their environmental impacts can be partially mitigated, that the proceedings can afford useful opportunities for public education, and that occasionally some of the most environmentally damaging timber plans and management alternatives can be blocked. Participation can also lay the groundwork for important legal challenges, which though expensive and time-consuming, can have far-reaching impacts. Whereas some activists are engaged in the National Forest planning process to improve the plans, others are involved to delay logging through the filing of lengthy administrative appeals, or as a necessary step in exhausting administrative remedies in order to clear the way for court challenges to the plans.

The fact that many important management decisions are made or reviewed in the Forest Service planning process is a good enough reason for many forest activists to participate (along with pursuing other forest protection activities) while recognizing that the whole process leaves much to be desired, given that its rules and regulations are set by the Forest Service, which therefore has a great deal of discretion as to which input to act upon. For those who want to become involved, the following general guidelines are offered.

Become intimately familiar with relevant administrative procedures governing plan reviews, public comments, and appeals processes, and study the relevant administrative rules governing public input for the planning process in which you intend to participate. Next, obtain copies of, or access to, all planning documents for the forest management plan or proposed timber harvest. Read them with the utmost care and scrutinize them in great detail for consistency with applicable NFMA rules and regulations. Attend public meetings at which documents are reviewed. Raise questions about anything you don't understand or agree with. Seek expert advice on critical points of forest ecology and environmental law. Communicate your concerns about the plans in writing by certified mail within relevant deadlines and talk directly about your concerns with representatives of the agencies involved. Your influence is probably greatest at the local level and closest to home. In the early stages, the completeness and correctness of every element of a local timber harvest plan are open to challenge.

Among the larger issues to consider at both the local and national level during plan review are compliance with environmental statutes, especially regarding endangered species and cumulative environmental impacts; logging practices, including timing of harvest; suitability of land for timber production; and timber removal prescriptions. You can also comment on the sizes of proposed withdrawal (no-cut) areas or special treatment areas, on regeneration practices, and on retention of snags and downed logs, as well as on such matters as logging equipment, roading, sedimentation, water temperature impacts on fisheries and amphibians, peak flow effects, and other aquatic impacts. You may propose alterations in the size of the area proposed for logging and the logging methods. You can also challenge the environmental assessment methods; the breadth, depth, and qualifications of the assessment personnel; and also whether feasible alternatives and mitigation have been adequately considered. Since lands that cannot be cut without irreversible damage to soils, productivity, or watershed, or that cannot be adequately restocked after logging, cannot legally be cut, you can also challenge national timber sales and plans on the suitability-for-harvest issue.

Once you have done your best to improve or stop a local timber harvest plan and the plan has nonetheless been approved, your involvement need not end. By informally monitoring the timber sale and compliance with any restrictions incorporated into it, including mitigation requirements, you can help assure that forest damage is kept to a minimum. Should you discover that sale conditions are not being observed by the timber operator, you can request inspections from the agency whose regulations are being violated or whose resources are affected.

To be effective in the public participation process for the National Forests, it may be helpful to have an overview of the Forest Service planning process. The opportunity for public involvement in the environmental impact statement (EIS) process begins with the publication of an announcement in the *Federal Register* of intent to prepare an EIS. The Forest Service then holds public participation activities, such as meetings, workshops, conferences, tours, and hearings, and will make its documents available through its principal offices (national headquarters, regional offices, forest supervisors' offices, district rangers' offices) and at other locations.

Public participation rhetoric notwithstanding, the public input to National Forest plans occurs in the context of a decision framework determined by Congress and senior Forest Service officials. Following completion of a national resource assessment called for by the RPA, each forest supervisor must estimate a range of possible timber production outputs for that forest corresponding to its resource capabilities and different logging rates. These outputs are aggregated to produce a range of national timber production outputs that are compared to an estimate of projected national timber demand. A top-down decision is then made by the Forest Service, subject to approval by Congress and the president, as to the overall timber output desired from the national forests. The total volume of timber desired is then divided into production quotas that are assigned to each of the Forest Service's nine forest regions. Within each region, portions of the quotas are reallocated to the individual forests within those regions.

Forest supervisors can challenge these quotas as inconsistent with local resource capabilities and can negotiate them with their regional forester if they believe that fulfillment of the quota will cause unacceptable environmental harm and impair the forest for other uses. Regional foresters, in turn, can negotiate assigned regional objectives with the chief forester of the Forest Service. In practice, it is not easy for quotas to be revised, and often, at best, excessive logging activities may merely be shifted from one National Forest to another.

Each forest plan is developed in a ten-step process that begins with the identification of salient issues and concerns. Citizen input is particularly useful in this formative stage as it serves to scope the planning effort and focus the entire impact assessment process. Other stages of the process include development of process and decision criteria; data collection (inventorying); resource capability analysis; and formulation of alternatives. The alternatives are supposed to be responsive to the issues and concerns raised in the initial scoping step. If they are not, at this stage citizens can suggest additional alternatives for inclusion in the analysis. Next, the impacts of each alternative are studied and evaluated, and a preferred alternative is selected that becomes the basis for the draft forest plan. A monitoring program is also developed. After affording a number of opportunities for public involvement during the steps described, the Forest Service produces its comprehensive draft forest plan and accompanying draft environmental impact statement (DEIS), which identify the Forest Service's preferred management alternative. Members of the public then usually have three months to provide written comments on the DEIS to the regional forester's office. The Forest Service reviews public comments on these drafts and responds to them in its final draft forest plan and EIS.

Decisions of all Forest Service officers can be appealed in sequence up the Forest Service chain of command. Those who are

dissatisfied with a forest plan following its final adoption can appeal it within forty-five days of the decision by filing a "Notice
of Appeal" with the regional forester along with a "Statement of
Reasons." A stay (delay) in implementation of the plan or particular management actions can also be requested, although the
Forest Service is not obligated to grant the stay. A request can
also be made for an appeal to be heard before the chief forester's
office. First, however, the regional forester will respond to the
appeal and will forward the appeal record to the chief forester
for a decision. If granted, the hearing will be informal and
affords an opportunity to discuss, negotiate, and settle both policy and site-specific issues without litigation and without need-
ing the presence of an attorney, although legal advice can be
valuable in formulating the arguments, especially if one antici-
pates ultimately taking the issues to court. Forest Service Regional Guides (management guidelines) can also be appealed,
but to the secretary of agriculture.

Readers who want more guidance on how to become involved in national and local forest planning should contact the
local and regional forest protection groups and alliances listed in
Appendix A. For a very valuable and still-relevant reference, see
*National Forest Planning: A Conservationist's Guide*, published in
1983 by The Wilderness Society, Sierra Club, Natural Resources
Defense Council, National Audubon Society, and National
Wildlife Federation. The Earth Justice Legal Defense Fund and
the Natural Resources Defense Council can provide you with assistance or referrals if you need legal advice on forest planning
issues.

CHAPTER 6

# FORESTRY AND
# LOGGING TECHNIQUES

Hurt not the earth, neither the sea, nor the trees.

The Book of Revelation

When we see land as a community to which we belong,
we may begin to use it with love and respect.

Aldo Leopold

Forestry is the management of a forested area and all of its resources. Forest stewardship is usually construed to include the protection of the forest's resources against fire, insects, disease, landslides, erosion, and avalanches. Industrial forestry as a distinctive type of forestry tends to operate on a capital-intensive agricultural model emphasizing commodity production of trees rather than protection of the forest as an ecological unit. To maximize the output of wood fiber per acre (for timber, pulp, or fuel), the industrial forester generally resorts to heavy machinery, chemical controls, and intensive management. Perpetuating a complete range of the natural forest's ecological processes is generally not a high priority in industrial forestry—so long as the absence of ecological health or diversity doesn't cost the landowner any timber revenue in the short term.

By contrast, sustainable forestry aims at delivering a continual yield of forest products by protecting the whole forest as an ecosystem and limiting extraction of its products to their incremental growth between cycles of extraction so that the forest is constantly able to renew itself without an overall loss in quantity or quality. Regularly taking more than the incremental growth is rather like deficit spending—a form of raiding the "capital," or stock, of forest products so that the ecosystem goes into decline over time. Yet both industrial and sustainable forestry include a common range of management goals, such as the production of timber, wildlife, water, fish, range, biodiversity, and recreation.

Ideally, forestry on anything but the smallest scale should follow a formal plan. A "forest management plan" explains the overall timber management strategy for a whole forest, such as even-age management (which requires clearcutting) or all-age management (which is compatible with selective cutting), and it outlines other management goals, such as the commodities and amenities to be obtained or protected, and the methods for accomplishing the goals. By contrast, a "timber harvest plan" (THP) describes a particular individual timber removal operation. Unfortunately, long-term forest plans are generally required only for the National Forests and for certain other federal lands, such as those of the Bureau of Land Management, as well as for large timber harvest operations in California. (On private lands in California, those long-term forest plans are referred to as "sustained yield plans.")

California's Forest Practices Act is widely regarded as the nation's strictest. It requires the preparation of a timber harvest plan for state and private industrial timber removal operations. Smaller ownerships (less than 2,500 acres) that secure an approved "nonindustrial timber management plan" (NTMP) are excused from preparing the more comprehensive THP. They are instead allowed to submit a "timber harvest notice" that briefly describes the proposed logging site and the operations to be conducted on it.

Despite its reputation as a rigorous regulatory framework, the act has major loopholes and is far too lenient to protect many forest ecosystems. For example, it excuses salvage logging operations from filing THPs. In recent years, the number of acres harvested under salvage exemptions has far exceeded the number harvested under conventional THPs. Moreover, even when a full THP is required, timber contractors at times inadvertently or intentionally fail to follow the plan's precise instructions. Sometimes, for example, the operator may accidentally cut the wrong trees or stray over the plan boundary. Culverts or other erosion control devices may be improperly installed and inadequately maintained. Within watercourse buffer zones, operators sometimes fail to maintain adequate controls on the use of heavy equipment, thereby allowing soil to enter waterways.

Outside California, Washington, and Oregon and Maine, which have less exacting forest protection laws than the former two states, forest management plans are ordinarily not required on private forest land, unless the land is enrolled with a public agency in a special forestry assistance or tax abatement program. Forest practice legislation and enforcement needs strengthening in most states, and citizen involvement is necessary to provide on-the-ground oversight to ensure that THP and other rules are followed. Although citizens are not allowed to trespass, they can often observe wrongdoing, file complaints, and alert the relevant permitting or other regulatory agency to the need for an immediate inspection.

Good forestry requires both a broad ecological knowledge of forests and related ecosystems as well as specific knowledge of logging technology, since forestry today is largely mechanized and computerized. For a large timber sale, the land is often surveyed from the air; the resulting photometric data are scanned into a computer and reproduced on a map. However, someone always "cruises" a representative portion of the timber sale area on foot to measure and assess it so that the yield of the logging operation can be accurately computed.

Where forest-level planning is required, the timber lessee or owner must submit a proposed forest management plan or THP to environmental review by the state or federal resource management agency in charge. The plan specifies the proposed timber removal method and related issues. If a significant environmental impact is deemed likely, an environmental impact statement (EIS) may be required, although in California, an approved THP is regarded as satisfying the requirements of the California Environmental Quality Act. Forest management plans for National Forest land and large California timber sales require a public review and comment period before logging permits can be granted. Environmental impacts are supposed to be mitigated under plan provisions.

If a timber operator wants to provide the forest with maximum protection and is not in a hurry to turn every last tree into money, timber can be extracted gradually from forests by selective cutting of individual trees. In a well-executed selective harvest, trees are felled precisely, sometimes with the help of jacks and cables, so as to minimize damage to trees left in the stand. Between the relatively light immediate physical impact of selective cutting and the extreme impact of clearcutting (discussed in detail in Chapter 8) lie various timber removal methods on a continuum of increasing impacts, from patch cuts to shelterwood cuts to seed tree cuts (see below).

## Logging Methods and Tools of the Trade

Good forestry requires the use of ecological knowledge, knowledge of logging techniques and silviculture, and site-specific judgment to match timber removal methods correctly with management goals and local conditions. In general, the ecological circumstances that justify removing a large portion of a forest's standing timber are few, although this approach is common in industrial forestry.

In industrial forestry, the size of the trees to be cut influences the choice of technology. Large trees are cut with chainsaws; on plantations of small trees, mobile logging machinery capable of seizing a whole tree trunk and cutting through it like a giant pruning shear is sometimes used. Once cut, the trees are handled in a variety of ways, depending on whether they are intended for lumber, pulp, or fuel, and on other factors, including the types, sizes, and quantities of trees. Thus, whereas some logging operations remove whole trees intended for use as power plant fuel, trees destined for the sawmill are typically limbed and topped by chainsaw and cut into sections. The limbs and tops are often left in the woods, and the trunks are dragged (skidded) or lifted out of the forest for loading on trucks. Sometimes, in preparing a tree for a pulp mill, the whole tree is limbed and topped on a landing. The bole might then be chipped and blown into a waiting truck.

Modern logging operations typically are highly mechanized. They use large, heavy equipment including Caterpillar-type (tracked) logging tractors, mobile yarders (a truck-mounted steel boom equipped with cables for dragging logs), bulldozers, log loaders, logging trucks, support vehicles for mechanical maintenance needs, and fixed-cable "yarding" machinery (to drag cut logs from the timber stand to the loading "yard").

## SELECTIVE CUTS

In a planned selective cut, certain trees are chosen for removal by a forester according to specific criteria derived from long-term forest management goals. For example, a simple strategy for improving a commercial timber stand is to remove defective and diseased trees to allow the remaining trees more room to grow. Another strategy is to harvest only trees that exceed a certain size and commercial value. Yet another strategy is to leave some of the largest and best trees standing to seed future generations. No matter what the selection strategy is, selective timber management generally requires the exercise of more judgment and skill than does wholesale tree removal. During a selective cut, care also must be taken not to injure the remaining trees, which might expose them to disease. For all these reasons, selective logging tends to be more labor-intensive than clearcutting, as well as because the forest needs to be reentered for successive cuts more frequently than with clearcuts. The use of selective cutting versus clearcutting may be especially necessary in hot, dry forests where unshaded seedlings might dry out and die following a clearcut or even a series of patch cuts. With selective cuts, the next generation of young trees will benefit from the shade cast by the remaining trees. Naturally, however, this tends to make the reestablishment of shade-intolerant species more difficult.

Despite its advantages, selective cutting is sometimes misapplied, resulting in "high grading"—removal of the best trees from the forest. This is akin to reverse genetic selection, with the worst, least commercially desirable trees left on site to seed the next generations. As the best trees are culled again and again over time, forest quality inexorably deteriorates. Another significant problem with selective cutting is that it is frequently used to cull all the commercially undesirable species from a forest, leaving nothing but a monoculture of the most marketable or valuable species, such as sugar maple. This result is known as "type conversion" or "stand conversion." Conversely, a timber operator might selectively remove all the commercially desirable trees, leaving only trees of low commercial value. Finally, because trees provide one another with protection against wind, sometimes the selective removal of trees can leave the remaining timber stand vulnerable to windthrow (toppling by wind). This is a concern on windy sites where thin soils prevent deep rooting.

Selective cutting may present a different kind of problem in areas that have serious infestations of root rot or bark beetles, or where most trees have been killed by fire or insects. By retaining sources of further infection, selective cutting may prolong infestations. If continued commercial timber production is the main goal in the short term, clearcutting may be necessary to control infestations, and the timber owner may also need to clearcut to salvage the dead timber en masse. Another forest-scale problem is the road building that may accompany selective cutting. Because much of the forest is left intact, more roads may be required to reach and remove the trees that are selectively cut than for other methods of tree removal, such as the patch cut. Much logging-related environmental damage to streams, fish, and water quality is directly attributable to roads, because of the erosion they cause. In good logging, timber operations are carefully planned to minimize the size and number of roads and to minimize their erosional impacts.

## PATCH CUTS

An alternative to selective cutting is the division of the forest into sections of equal size known as blocks and the sequential cutting of the blocks at regular intervals, leaving a patchwork of open spaces surrounded by forest. Each even-age patch of timber will form part of a distribution of age groups from young to older trees across the forest landscape. As each block reaches the age at which cutting has been prescribed, the patches are cut one after the other and replanted sequentially. The goal is to create a stratified age-class distribution of stands in the forest so that the timber volume taken in each cut is replaced by new growth of the younger forest blocks. This simplification of the forest's age structure allows a constant yield of commercially marketable timber to be taken from the forest periodically. While the timber acreage is eventually evenly apportioned among a range of age groups (classes), the distribution pattern of the trees, segregated by age across the landscape, is highly unnatural.

Still, a patch-cut forest is likely to be environmentally preferable to a clearcut, because the patch-cut forest contains trees of different ages versus the uniform age of trees regrowing in a clearcut forest. Patch cutting therefore also permits more forest heterogeneity as it allows some young, intermediate, and old habitat to remain available to wildlife while the next swath of forest grows to harvestable size. The usefulness to wildlife of the residual forest, however, depends on the size, shape, age, and connectedness of the forest fragments that remain.

A major disadvantage of patch cutting is the "edge effects" it creates, where forest meets grassland or newly exposed clearcut. By excising a four-sided block of trees from a forest, for example, a patch cut exposes the remaining forest on all four sides to wind, drying, and invasive species. Large numbers of adjacent bare patches also fragment the remaining forest habitat and impair the survival of some interior forest species, especially migratory songbirds in eastern U.S. forests.

The creation of new forest edges, for example, provides the brown-headed cowbird with an opportunity to destroy populations of smaller songbirds by laying its own eggs in their nests. Cowbird chicks hatch sooner and are larger than their songbird hosts and outcompete their songbird nestlings for food. Native to open country, the cowbird normally ranges only half a mile into closed forests. But new forest edges make large additional territory available to the cowbird, to the songbirds' detriment.

## SHELTERWOOD CUTS

A shelterwood cut removes most of the forest area's trees but leaves a thinned overstory to protect young seedlings from over-exposure to sun, wind, frost, or a combination of these influences. The overstory improves seedling establishment and growth by modifying their microclimate. Once the new generation of trees grows large enough not to need extra protection, loggers return to remove the older shelterwood canopy. This then leaves an even-age tree plantation, so shelterwood cutting is essentially a clearcut performed in stages. As such, it has most of the drawbacks of a clearcut.

## SEED TREE CUTS

A seed tree cut resembles a clearcut even more closely than does a shelterwood cut. All trees are removed except a few mature ones, which are left to provide seed for regeneration of a new tree crop. The seed trees provide little in the way of shelter and once their purpose has been accomplished, loggers typically reenter the site to remove them, leaving an even-age collection of seedlings or young saplings.

The industrial forestry procedures described here—selective cutting, shelterwood cutting, seed tree cutting, patch cutting, and clearcutting—while common in the West, vary greatly from region to region and across ecosystems. In the case of northeastern hardwoods held in small-scale private ownership, for example, trees are rarely clearcut for a number of reasons that render clearcutting economically and silviculturally unjustified. Instead of containing towering species with thick trunks and relatively condensed crowns, such as Douglas fir, redwood, Sitka spruce, or ponderosa pine, a stand of northeastern hardwoods might consist of many crowded, relatively thin-stemmed trees. Due to the high relative ratio of tree top-to-bole volume, limbing all but the largest specimens (as would probably be required after clearcutting) would not be cost-effective. Next, the small size of the landholding, the owner's presumed lack of capital or short planning horizons, plus the presence of difficult (broken) or mountainous terrain might make the use of expensive heavy machinery infeasible. Finally, even if clearcuts were made, hardwood planting generally produces poor results, and the creation of large, clearcut forest openings would invite predation on the new seedlings by white-tailed deer and rabbits.

Perhaps ten or fifteen years after tree planting, loggers return to a site for what is called "precommercial thinning." Trees and shrubs competing with the chosen specimens of desired species are cut down. Finally, at a time when, according to calculations based on timber growth rates, the standing timber has reached a volume that maximizes the owner's return on investment (or sooner if ready cash is needed), trees are once again cut. If the final operation is a clearcut, the whole cycle starts over. Generally, the more often this is done and the shorter the rotational period, the smaller are the trees produced.

## HERBICIDES AND OTHER BRUSH CONTROL METHODS

Next to clearcutting, the most controversial forestry topic is probably the use of herbicides to control brush and weeds that compete with trees. Plant competition can be so severe, in fact, that it can prevent tree establishment or make growth slow and survival problematic. Because herbicides are effective control agents and can be cheaply applied to the forest by air, they are economically attractive to forest managers. Environmentalists are generally arrayed against foresters on the subject of herbicides. Many professional foresters believe that the broadscale application of herbicides is safe for wildlife, humans, and commercial tree species. They contend that scientific evidence indicates that low-dose applications of herbicides do not make wildlife ill, kill soil organisms, damage soil structure, or bioaccumulate in animal tissue.

Following their application, herbicides are rapidly absorbed by vegetation or adsorbed onto soil and dust, where they are soon deactivated. Herbicide effects on a particular site depend on the compound's toxicity, persistence, mobility in soil, potential for bioaccumulation (if any), exposure pathways, and consequent exposure risks. Although laws and regulations prohibit the discharge of herbicides into surface water, an unintended infusion of herbicides into streams and wetlands can easily occur if a heavy rain falls soon after spraying; if an accidental spill takes place; if wind gusts carry spray from aircraft onto water; or if equipment and containers are emptied into waterways during cleaning. In high concentrations, herbicides can damage or destroy fish and other aquatic life and produce illness in humans. Nowadays, much more care is taken in the application of herbicides than in previous decades. Spraying is usually done during dry weather to prevent contamination of runoff, for example. However, personnel who spray herbicides on forest land are not necessarily trained or licensed. There is no federal licensing controlling herbicide application on private land, and regulations vary from county to county and state to state.

The effects of herbicides on soil are complex. Because herbicides kill broad-leafed vegetation, they cause an increase in the availability of nutrients released from the vegetation's dead and ruptured cells. Depending on climate and when new vegetation gets established, excess nutrients may then be leached from the soil by precipitation and lost to plant roots. Spraying kills broad-leafed native species of trees and shrubs, such as alder and cean-othus, which are natural soil repair agents. These plants host nitrogen-fixing bacteria attached to their roots. The bacteria enrich the soil with soluble nitrogen suitable for plant uptake. When tree and shrub roots that support fungi are killed, the microflora of the forest soil changes, and the fungal community and the organisms that live upon it are reduced. In its stead, the bacterial population of the soil increases, along with a more bacteria-dependent food web.

Despite astute public relations by defoliant manufacturers and timber companies, some phenoxy herbicides widely used by timber companies can be dangerous to humans and wildlife. One phenoxy herbicide in particular—2,4,5,T—was implicated in cancer, blood disorders, rashes, miscarriages, and birth defects. Aside from its intrinsic toxicity, 2,4,5,T during its manufacture was also frequently contaminated with dioxin, an ultratoxic compound. Since the use of Agent Orange in Vietnam aroused public concerns about herbicide effects, some of the more toxic and persistent herbicides have been taken off the market. Today, 2,4,5,T is banned in the United States. The closely related compound 2,4,D is still legal in the United States, but those who apply it must be trained and certified. Moreover, because of the 2,4,5,T controversy, 2,4,D is no longer used in California.

The U.S. Forest Service is a major user of herbicides and, according to the U.S. Department of Agriculture, in 1994 applied 86,000 pounds of herbicides, algaecides, and plant growth regulators for purposes ranging from site preparation to weed control to conifer release. Among the most heavily used herbicides were 2,4,D alone and in combination with other compounds, glyphosate, Picloram, and Triclopyr.

Herbicide application is only one of many methods that can reduce competing vegetation. All have their pros and cons. Whereas manual control of brush (by hand labor) eliminates the tops of plants, the roots and shoots survive in the soil to resprout later. From the standpoint of forest preservation, this is a benefit, but the brush then competes with commercial trees for space, light, nutrients, and moisture. In contrast to the manually controlled plant, the roots of the herbicide-treated plant die and cease to compete with the trees. That is just what the commercial forester wants.

If instead of using hand labor, brush control is done with heavy, mechanized equipment, it may compact soil, harm tree roots, and cause erosion. Manual brush control does not have these disadvantages, but is much more labor-intensive and likely to require repeat treatments. In some cases where native brush is thick, it may be ripped out by bulldozer and brush rake. The ground may then be harrowed with a heavy-duty scarification plow to open it for planting. Although manual brush control is invariably less damaging to the land, mechanized or herbicidal brush control is usually adopted because these methods are cheaper.

Prescribed burning is another alternative to herbicides. Whereas forest burning does not introduce synthetic toxins into the environment, it can deplete soil nutrients by destroying organic matter (humus) in the soil and by oxidizing nitrogen during combustion. Burning is also sometimes used to dispose of logging debris. Grazing is widely used to manage low-growing vegetation, but may have some undesirable ecological effects. Sheep and cattle can damage desirable species and introduce diseases to wildlife.

As noted, good forestry depends on the choice of appropriate silvicultural and harvesting methods combined with a thorough understanding of forest ecology and a knowledge of the requirements of the tree species being grown and harvested. Good forestry also requires a continuous and enduring commitment to the land following logging to ensure long-term erosion control and long-term survival of regeneration plantings. Roads and drainages often require maintenance over long periods of time to prevent uncontrolled erosion, including landslides and damage to natural watercourses.

# CHAPTER 7

# OF OLD GROWTH, SPOTTED OWLS, AND SALVAGE LOGGING

Love the forest. Appreciate the forest. Give thanks that
the forest sustains us.

Herb Hammond, *Seeing the Forest among the Trees*

The fate of old-growth forests and the northern
spotted owl in the Pacific Northwest has been the
focus of a bitter and longstanding dispute between
environmentalists and the timber industry. In response to environmentalists' challenges in U.S. District Court to
old-growth forest logging under the Endangered Species Act,
U.S. District Judge William L. Dwyer ruled in 1991 that the federal government had failed to protect the spotted owl as required
by law. He therefore issued a comprehensive ban on further logging on federal forests until their management plans were
brought into compliance with the Endangered Species Act. This
and prior decisions virtually halted logging of the ancient
forests on federal lands for more than five years.

To meet conditions set by Judge Dwyer, the federal government convened a special study group in 1993 to assist it in re-
solving the Pacific Northwest forest crisis. Known as the Forest
Ecosystem Management Assessment Team (FEMAT), the group

was directed to use an "ecosystem approach" in delineating forest management alternatives. FEMAT's efforts cost more than $3 million and, including its subteams and fourteen advisory subgroups, utilized the services of 600 to 700 people. The team gathered and assessed scientific evidence regarding the biology and survival prospects of the owl and developed candidate alternative policies for the management of the more than 24 million acres of federally owned forest land in Oregon and Washington.

Then, at a high-level forest conference on April 2, 1993, in Portland, Oregon, President Clinton committed his administration to the goal of crafting a balanced, comprehensive, scientifically sound, ecologically credible, legally responsible, long-term forest management solution to the conflict. In July 1993, when FEMAT produced its analysis and outlined ten possible management options, the Clinton administration announced its "Forest Plan for a Sustainable Economy and a Sustainable Environment," based on Option 9 of the FEMAT alternatives. Many forest activists opposed Option 9 for not protecting all spotted owl habitat and for creating old-growth reserves that are not sustainable. Proindustry critics have assailed the plan for protecting too much owl habitat.

After an environmental impact statement (EIS) was done, the forest plan was formally presented to Judge Dwyer on April 14, 1994. The EIS requires that any logging must be done consistent with certain ecosystem management criteria. These criteria require that the effects of timber operations on endangered species must be considered in the aggregate across the entire landscape of old-growth timber holdings on federal lands in the Northwest. Examining the effects of logging on a particular local site would not be sufficient to meet this test. To make the reduction in federal timber supplies more palatable, the president promised a $1.2 billion economic aid package for the affected region over a five-year period. The plan went into effect on a limited basis in 1994 and provided for the resumption of some logging in the Northwest's old-growth forests, but at levels far below those of the 1980s.

In July 1995, to the profound dismay of environmentalists, President Clinton—despite his own avowed objections—reluctantly signed into law a $16.3 billion spending bill with a totally unrelated rider containing logging provisions he had previously vetoed. The new law specifically exempted salvage timber sales in the National Forests of the Pacific Northwest from federal environmental laws, such as the Endangered Species Act and the Clean Water Act, and barred citizens from challenging the salvage sales in court. Characterized by supporters as "emergency legislation," the new provisions doubled "salvage logging" rates on federal lands damaged or threatened by fire, disease, or insects. Moreover, the new law defined "salvage" logging so broadly that industry argued that up to a billion board feet of healthy, live timber could be cut under the legislation. Depending on the field conditions justifying the sale, salvage logging may be done by selective cutting or by other techniques. Whereas "salvage logging" rates were to be doubled in damaged federal forests, the bill also expedited logging on vast healthy forests that provide spotted owl habitat. Sierra Club representatives said the new bill dismantled the administration's much-touted Pacific Northwest Forest Plan and increased logging activity.

Salvage-logging controversies have not been confined to the Northwest. The Lake Tahoe Basin Management Unit (a unit within the National Forest System) in northern California, for example, contains a rapidly deteriorating fire-prone forest comprised largely of dying fir trees, with some native pine. Like many contemporary forest problems, it is a legacy of earlier mistreatment.

Located not far from the shores of scenic Lake Tahoe, the trees were weakened by six years of drought and, by the summer of 1995, were quickly succumbing to two of their ancient insect enemies: the pine bark beetle and the fir engraver. Lake Tahoe, the deepest and largest mountain lake in North America, was also one of America's clearest before extensive development in its basin. Visibility in the lake is declining rapidly now—by a third in less than forty years—due to excessive nutrients that to a large extent enter the lake on eroded soil particles. (Construction of buildings, roads, and trails, as well as logging, are principal causes of soil erosion.)

Before the Gold Rush, the lake shores had been cloaked in a magnificent, fire-resistant forest of tall and well-spaced pines: reddish ponderosa, vanilla-scented Jeffreys, gray lodgepoles, and thick-barked sugar pines with giant cones. Periodic fires had kept the more susceptible firs in check on the forest floor. But once the valuable pines in the watershed were clearcut for mine timbers or charcoal and a period of fire suppression began, a crowded, predominantly fir forest emerged. Citing the possibility of an uncontrollable wildfire in the Lake Tahoe Basin Management Unit, the Forest Service decided to rely on commercial logging, rather than controlled burns, to manage the unhealthy forest. In the greater Tahoe area (outside the lake basin itself), Sierra Pacific Industries, among other companies, bought the right to cut dead and dying timber in a salvage operation that allows the cutting of some surviving pine trees that are overdense and susceptible to disease and crown fires. Neither logging too near the lake nor a catastrophic wildfire, however, is good for Lake Tahoe, since both cause polluting runoff. The ecological integrity of both forest and lake must be protected. Hopefully, managers of the Tahoe National Forest will insist on the highest standards of forest management for the region, resisting temptations to rely primarily on commercial logging, which might not protect and enhance the area's extraordinary ecological values.

Salvage logging as practiced in reality often contrasts with the high-minded ecological rationales used to justify it. For example, the Forest Service authorized an extensive salvage logging of 130 million board feet in the Boise National Forest in Idaho following a 1992 fire. The logging was ostensibly to restore the forest's health, and on its completion, the Forest Service expressed satisfaction with the quality of the work. No environmental impact statement or administrative review had been required. But after months of investigation and on-site inspection, environmental activists found that logging operations had been conducted in off-limits zones, "healthy trees were improperly cut . . . damaged lands were not properly replanted," creeks with imperiled species were adversely impacted, and helicopter landing pads were built beside sensitive streams.

Timber industry lobbyists and their allies in Congress sought legislation in 1996 to extend the temporary salvage-logging legislation and make it permanent. Fortunately, their efforts failed, and the rider mercifully expired.

# CHAPTER 8

# CLEARCUTTING

> Clearcutting might be economically efficient, but the attempts to justify it with ecological arguments fall short. . . . Soil nutrients are depleted when the entire [above ground] forest biomass is carried off on a logging truck or burned in the aftermath of a clearcut.
>
> Ray Raphael, *Tree Talk*

 No forestry topic evokes stronger emotions than clearcutting. Clearcutting is the removal of all trees on a site and the consequent loss of forest conditions, such as the influences of the forest canopy and roots on the soil and forest floor. Environmentalists generally abhor clearcutting. Foresters and commercial timber operators use it frequently and regard it as a legitimate forest management practice. The debate often obscures two separate and important issues. The first is whether a particular site should be logged at all; the second is, if the logging is acceptable or necessary, what logging method is appropriate for the site? Taking these issues into consideration, this chapter explores why clearcuts are done, what their effects are, and when they are warranted.

Most large commercial timber companies find it more profitable to clearcut coniferous forest than to log selectively. (Hardwoods are more frequently logged selectively, as discussed in Chapter 6.) Since clearcutting creates a uniform habitat, it allows a timber operator to control brush and replant efficiently. Timber management activities, such as thinning and herbicide treatments, can be efficiently conducted after clearcutting to reestablish the next generation of trees. The size of a clearcut and rotation length (the time between clearcuts on the same parcel) are critical to assessing the clearcut's ecological impact. A patch cut the length and width of a mature tree, for example, creates an opening in the forest that natural forest processes can readily fill. A clearcut of more than 20 acres, however, creates a sudden forest void that is much more difficult for the forest to repair.

Various costs and the projected net revenues of a clearcut versus those of a selective cut are weighed by a timber company contemplating clearcutting. The first obvious economic incentive for clearcutting is that more salable trees can be taken to market right away at the same time. Even though more trees are cut than in a selective cut, the clearcutting operation might be less expensive, since no effort need be expended to select trees and protect them during removal of their neighbors. In a coniferous forest, however, reforestation after a clearcut may be more costly than reforestation after selective cutting. (This would not be true, however, in cutting hardwoods that naturally regenerate by resprouting from stumps.) The higher costs of regeneration in a softwood-dominated forest are due to the fact that clearcutting removes all trees, whereas in selective cuts, young trees of intermediate sizes and ages are left standing and have a head start on newly planted seedlings. On a clearcut site, therefore, a timber manager must wait longer to the next commercial harvest than with a selection cut.

Clearcutting is also attractive to timber companies because it produces trees of the same age in the generation following the cut. Their management is convenient for timber companies, because forest operations can be done concurrently throughout an even-age site, and clearcutting makes it possible to produce a new generation of trees of uniform size and quality that are easier to mill. While the motives behind clearcutting are usually economic, *once a decision has been made to log a forest*, sound ecological arguments can *in some instances* be made for managing by clearcutting versus other tree removal methods. What are these circumstances?

## When Clearcutting *May* Be Warranted

Commercial foresters recommend the use of clearcutting for salvaging logs from forests killed by insects or fire and when extensive root disease or infestation by dwarf mistletoe exists. Failure to remove the diseased or infested material may lead to rapid transmission of insects or diseases to the next generation of trees. Clearcutting may also be necessary for the removal of single-species stands of invasive exotic trees, such as eucalyptus. If the goal is to convert the area from eucalyptus to native trees, it would make no sense to selectively cut the eucalyptus. Because of the vigor with which eucalyptus grows and reproduces, the area would soon again be covered with eucalyptus.

Arguments also can be made for clearcutting relatively flat and erosion-resistant temperate land that was previously planted with commercially managed single-age, single-species trees. Such lands already resemble plantations or farms more than forests and, so long as there is no real prospect of their restoration to forest, and so long as their soils are not damaged by abuse, most of the harm has already been done by the initial forest removal operation. As is explained later, however, the decision to grow trees in these monocultures makes them more susceptible to insects and pathogens.

Timber managers wanting to grow a species that requires direct sun for establishment or for vigorous growth may also opt for clearcutting and attempt to justify their decision on ecological grounds, whereas the underlying motivation is basically economic. The industry contends that forest clearing is necessary to establish certain shade-intolerant species, such as Douglas fir. This assumption, however, does not justify clearcutting. Openings in a forest canopy can be made for new plantings by selective cutting, and Douglas fir will grow there, just as new firs sprout naturally in sunny patches of forest floor when a mature fir tree falls. Granted, the new fir recruits will be fewer in number when forced to compete for light and space than if the entire area had been cleared. Patch cutting as the chosen alternative to clearcutting, however, entails an ecological price due to forest fragmentation and edge effects, as discussed elsewhere.

Many hard-to-regenerate forests are, in industry's view, also candidates for clearcutting. These sites include so called "stagnant forests." The stagnant forest is a climax forest that has been undisturbed for many centuries in cool, wet, northern climates and may be undergoing deterioration associated with old age and the long-term absence of natural disturbances. Because of large forest litter accumulations and the slow rate at which litter decomposes under cold conditions, soils become acidified and simultaneously insulated from summer warmings. The effects can be the eventual degradation of the soil into permafrost and very slow forest growth. In the past, foresters have advocated clearcutting such forests, but poor regeneration often results. Ecologists argue that whereas these forests may be stagnant from an economic point of view, they should be protected and studied, because we know little about their ecological processes and the species dependent on those processes.

## When Clearcutting Should Not Be Used

Even foresters who might sanction clearcutting as an acceptable industrial forestry technique recognize that it is totally inappro-

priate on steep, unstable mountainsides where erosion, landslides, or avalanches are a problem. Nor should clearcutting be
done in high-elevation subalpine forests where the "thermal island effect" of tree trunks is required for good seedling establishment. In general, forests situated in any harsh climate—for
example, very hot and dry, or frost-prone lands—need forest
cover for successful regeneration and likewise should not be
clearcut. Nor should drainages be clearcut if they are dissected
by many small streams susceptible to siltation and nutrient over-
enrichment. Whereas buffer strips can be created along larger
streams and rivers, streams and wetlands may be so numerous
and pervasive in some areas that buffering is impractical. Naturally, these areas, too, should not be clearcut. Clearcutting also
should not be done where it will deprive endangered species of
needed continuous forest cover, or where the visual impact of
the cut will be a blight on the land.

## The Case against Clearcutting

Many, if not most, environmentalists believe that no valid ecological argument can justify completely removing a forest or
large timber stand in a single operation. This view usually rests
on a love and respect for nature and is often passionately held.
Adherents of this position are unlikely to alter their convictions.
Nor would a lumber mill owner likely relinquish the belief that
the transformation of forests to lumber by the most efficient
means available is in society's best interest. Beyond these polar-
ized positions—the environmentalist's fundamental belief in
forest preservation and the lumberman's utilitarian attitude—two
basic and pragmatic kinds of important objections to clearcutting need to be considered. The first is based on the kind of forest to be logged; the second type pertains to the damage
clearcutting does.

Regarding the first objection, opponents of clearcutting maintain that it should not be used to eliminate increasingly scarce old-growth forest. In the space of a few hours or days, a clearcut can destroy old-growth ecosystems that may have taken millennia to develop. Once old growth is cut, it will not return for hundreds of years, if ever. As to the second objection, critics of clearcutting maintain that it permanently damages forests so that they will be unable to produce sustained yields of timber after one or more cycles of clearcutting. The science of forest ecology offers us some insights into these issues.

Forest ecology teaches that nature at times brusquely disrupts and even destroys forests by hurricane, tornado, earthquake, avalanche, volcanic eruption, fire, flood, disease, insect infestations, and combinations of these events and processes. This is not to say that clearcutting mimics natural processes. Whereas natural catastrophes in forests may *kill* trees, they rarely *remove* trees en masse from the forest. However, forests have evolved the capability of regenerating following even violent catastrophic events. Thus, as disruptive as clearcutting is to forest processes, *under certain circumstances and given sufficient time*, nature is quite capable of repairing local damage and of recreating a mature intact forest. The fears about forest health and welfare following clearcutting are in these cases essentially fears about forests' recuperative powers.

Some clearcut lands will naturally regenerate rapidly as forest, especially the highly productive lands in regions of ample rainfall, such as the Pacific Northwest. Adjacent undamaged forests and the soil bank of the clearcut site then serve as sources of seed. Lower-quality timber land, however, may not regenerate after a clearcut and may require expensive and problematic reforestation efforts. Recovery after clearcutting depends on a number of site-specific factors, since its impacts depend on where, when, and how it is done. (The "how" refers not only to the tree-felling and log removal methods, but also to the clearcut's size and shape.) Clearcutting unquestionably has complex effects on soil, water, wildlife, microclimate, and biodiversity. Some of these effects act upon one another to compound forest damage.

Once a site has been clearcut and replanted with one or a few species, diversity is greatly reduced. Habitats and ecological niches for a vast variety of creatures are eliminated. Their losses in turn affect the populations of the species dependent on them, and the damage cascades through the ecosystem and beyond. Through clearcutting, the complex natural forest is reduced to a much simplified system of a single, or very few, species. This monoculture (or near-monoculture) is ultimately more susceptible to attack by disease and pests than natural forest. Without old standing dead trees, for example, woodpeckers that normally thrive on forest insects will be virtually absent from the new plantation, so a bark beetle invasion may wreck havoc on the new trees. Because all the trees are the same age and similar in height, the movement and reproduction of insects and disease from tree to tree is easier and quicker. Because the trees are grown in full sunlight, they may have more branches (depending on spacing) than those grown in the partial shade of a forest canopy, and therefore will be of lower quality for lumber.

Deforestation exposes the ground directly to sun, wind, and rain. It therefore modifies the humidity, light, temperature, and wind speed affecting the seedlings. The seedlings are therefore exposed to a harsher environment, with more extremes of temperature—both heat and frost—moisture and drying, and wind. Isolated individual clearcuts do not significantly affect climate, but their cumulative effects may do so. Moisture transpired by trees humidifies the atmosphere and can contribute to cloud formation or intensify rainfall. Deforestation of thousands of square miles—as in the tropics, and in the United States due to fire—can also affect regional climate by influencing the reflectance of the Earth's surface and the carbon dioxide concentration of the atmosphere.

The heavy logging equipment often used in clearcutting tends to disturb and compact the soil. Compaction makes it harder for tree roots to penetrate the soil and reduces soil pore spaces, which contain oxygen needed by soil microorganisms that make organic and inorganic matter available for uptake by trees and other vegetation. Once land is stripped of trees and other ground cover, their roots no longer hold soil in place. Sloping clearcut sites are then vulnerable to rapid erosion and slope failure after heavy rains. Erosion damage also affects streams and rivers, where heavy loads of silt and debris in runoff clog spawning gravels. Eventually, silt in streambeds can raise stream levels, cause floods, and undercut banks. That, in turn, can cause landslides, adding even greater sediment loads to streams. Raised to new heights by sediment in their channels, flood-stage streams can then undermine and topple even giant trees in the flood plain. Disturbance can also be translocated farther downstream as sediment and debris move in the streambed to the lower elevations of the watershed.

Bereft of trees, a landscape may lose more of its precipitation to runoff. Stream flow may then become more seasonally variable, prone to high flows in spring and low flows during the summer dry season. Water quality may be affected if suspended sediment and nutrient loads are increased through erosion. Loss of forest cover to clearcutting also exposes the ground to warming earlier in the spring, leading to earlier and more complete melting of snowpacks. This can lead to a spring flush or spate of water instead of a steadier flow of longer duration. In winter, loss of tree cover that kept snow shallow in spots may make it harder for deer and elk to find food in early spring.

Just as erosion removes nutrients, back on the logging site,

the soil's nutrient capital is further reduced by the physical removal of the cut tree trunks and frequently by the burning or removal of slash. The most serious effects are caused by whole tree
removal. Less harm is done to the soil's nutrient bank if
branches and tree tops are left on site to help rebuild the soil.
Not only does the woody debris provide habitat for wildlife that
play important roles in nutrient cycling and seed dispersal, but
logs and other large chunks of decaying, downed wood also
serve the forest as "slow-release fertilizer."

Some effects of clearcutting can be mitigated by leaving
quantities of downed wood on the ground after the cut to help
soil recovery and provide wildlife habitat. Similarly, snags (dead,
broken, and misshapen trees) should be left standing for cavity-
nesting birds. While these snags and logging debris may look
untidy, they are ecologically useful. In National Forests, the
number of snags left per acre is prescribed in timber harvest
plans.

## Minimizing Damage When Removing Trees
## (from Both Clearcuts and Selective Cuts)

Since much of the damage from logging is caused by roads and
yarding areas, selective cutting may not be the method of choice
in steep mountain areas or elsewhere. Ground-based logging
under selection silviculture usually requires an extensive network
of temporary roads, known as skid trails, on which logs are
dragged out of the woods, usually by Caterpillar tractors. This
equipment, when used on certain soils and under certain conditions, may cause severe damage to the roots of remaining trees.
Although other log removal methods exist, they, too, have environmental costs, and not all of the alternative systems are compatible with selective cutting operations.

Specialized and gentler logging methods exist than simply

dragging a tree out of the woods by tractor. While horses do less damage to the woods, they are not powerful enough to remove the largest logs. In some areas, trees are removed on top of the snow to minimize damage. Lifting logs out by helicopter minimizes damage to the soil and other trees but is costly (up to $40,000 a day). In addition, it consumes thousands of gallons of fossil fuel a day; requires cleared landing pads; and is easily restricted by rain and fog.

"Balloon logging" uses a balloon instead of a helicopter to suspend the logs in the air, but like cable and skyline yarding, it requires cable rigging to guide the balloon. "Skyline yarding," or the suspension of logs entirely off the ground from an aerial cable system, reduces ground damage but roughly doubles the cost of tractor logging as it requires the frequent rerigging of cables each time operations move through a timber stand. "High-lead yarding" suspends only one end of the log off the ground by an elevated cable on a boom or spar and drags the other on the ground to a landing area. "Cable yarding" requires large landing areas and wider roads for mobile yarders than for trucks, as well as the nonselective cutting of trees beneath each cable to facilitate passage of the logs. Both cable and balloon systems cause much less damage to the ground than dragging the logs along skid trails, but they are difficult or impractical to operate on selective cuts because of the obstruction of the remaining forest. A compromise solution sometimes used is to clearcut "alleys" within the logging area along which cables are set. Because of the erosion that cable logging can produce on steep, forested slopes, it is not always preferable to tractor logging. And because nonselective cutting may be inappropriate on some sites, there is no panacea.

In short, no logging method known is without environmental impacts. Contrary to what one might expect, if cable yarding and helicopters are disqualified for a particular steep site, a clearcut might do less soil damage than selective skidding of logs on a multitude of trails. However, if the slope is so steep and the soil so unstable that erosion from skid trails would be a problem, clearcutting is probably ill-advised as well, and the site should not be logged at all.

## Site Preparation and Replanting After Clearcutting

Clones of a single conifer species are often planted in the ground following clearcutting, converting the site to a commercial forest. As part of the process, the ground may be treated with herbicides to suppress all broad-leafed plants and hardwoods that would compete with the desired commercial tree crop or that might harbor rodents that eat seedlings. The alternative of simply clearing brush in small patches immediately around seedlings is generally rejected by timber managers because of the speed with which uncontrolled native brush can invade from the surrounding area. What's good for a single-species tree crop may not be good for the forest or its wildlife, however. Apart from its effects on the soil, elimination of brush species deprives wildlife of forage, berries, seeds, and cover. Foresters who clearcut generally make a number of optimistic assumptions. They posit that the roots of native brush will survive all but the most intensive removal operations; that wildlife will eventually reinvade from adjoining areas; and that soil organisms and the soil fertility dependent on them will naturally recover. These assumptions may easily prove flawed, to varying degrees, especially when the cumulative impacts of clearcutting within a region are considered over time.

During the establishment of a commercial tree crop, young seedlings may need to be protected against predators. In some cases, the industrial forester's solution is to control small mammals, such as gophers or mountain beavers, by poisoning or trapping. The bark of young commercial species is also sometimes coated with distasteful or toxic chemicals. Deer and elk hunting may be deliberately increased in the area to reduce browsing. Initially, these species may naturally increase in numbers in and around clearcuts and patchcuts as more sunlight on the forest floor stimulates the development of succulent new growth, but when monocultures of trees become well established and the now homogeneous forest canopy closes, the resulting habitat is less generally desirable for them in the long run than before logging. Historically, many commercial forestry operations have shown minimal regard for wildlife, soil fertility, native plants, or erosion, and tend to ignore the roles of soil organisms, small forest animals, and other noncommercial "components" of the forest ecosystem. Those organisms, however, are important to soil aeration and to soil nutrient and water-holding capacity.

Following clearcutting and the extensive erosion that often occurs on slopes, the initial planting of tree seed or seedlings may fail to thrive. Then, without the shelter of trees to shade it and to slow evaporation, the impoverished soil may dry out and be overgrown with brush. This is enough to greatly delay the reestablishment of healthy forest.

When followed by replanting, clearcutting is in essence an attempt by foresters to skip the normal successional processes that nature developed to take the forest progressively from natural catastrophe back to ecological climax vegetation. With the planting of preselected trees after clearcutting and the extirpation of competing native vegetation and a whole spectrum of other life essential to a healthy forest, logging sites are not allowed to repair themselves naturally and replenish their lost nutrients so as to ensure the forest's reestablishment and long-term survival. Cyclical clearcutting and associated management practices are likely to produce steady forest degradation, with unpredictable long-term environmental consequences. Successive clearcutting is therefore not a sustainable process with respect to maintainence of soil quality or tree yields. The deleterious effects, however, may take three or more generations of clearcutting to become obvious. Since forestry itself has been practiced for only a relatively few generations of trees, much of the inevitable harm is not yet apparent.

In the forests of Germany, where professional forestry had its beginnings in the late eighteenth century, the planting of conifer stands and their clearcutting on "short rotation" (at frequent intervals) was widely adopted by landowners attracted by the possibilities of short-term economic gain from fast-growing softwoods. The short rotation on those pine and spruce forests was not unlike the rotation periods used on commercial forests in North America today. Writing in *The Forest and the Trees: A Guide to Excellent Forestry,* the late Gordon Robinson, a forester and proponent of sustainable forestry, described what this practice accomplished in Germany in only a century and a quarter:

> Deciduous hardwoods and true fir became nearly extinct . . . By the time of the First World War it had become clearly apparent that something was very wrong. Trees were stunted; many died before they even approached the size of the original forest trees. Soils had become impoverished, and trees suffered increasingly from storms, insects, and diseases.

This is the *direction* in which short-rotation, single-species, commercial tree cropping is heading in the United States, too. Could we be making the same mistakes with our forests that the Europeans made with theirs a hundred years ago? Some of the economic forces driving us in this direction are described in the following chapter.

# CHAPTER 9

# FORESTS, MONEY, AND JOBS

The [timber] companies had been quietly trimming
payrolls for decades as advancing technologies made
labor-saving possible.

Alan Thein Durning,
*Saving the Forests: What Will It Take?*

Three years into a drastic curtailment of logging in
Federal forests, Oregon, the top timber-producing state,
has posted its lowest unemployment rate in a
generation, just over 5 percent. What was billed as an
agonizing choice of jobs versus owls has proved to be
neither, thus far.

Timothy Egan, *New York Times*,
October 11, 1994

## Good Forestry Is Rare

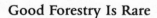

Timber company managers are motivated to keep
timber company owners and investors happy by
maximizing owners' equity and by boosting the
company's stock price, if it is a public company. Apart from
obeying the laws of the land, timber managers—with some

laudable exceptions—are apt to pay little attention to the health of the forest ecosystem, its wildlife, fisheries, and watershed, unless protecting those resources happens to be part of their company's management plan.

The same incentives that militate against moderate cutting also deter forest restoration. The forest owner who is only interested in monetizing the timber resource and regards the forest mainly as a capital asset in an investment portfolio is not motivated to perpetuate the forest when doing so reduces apparent profits. Businesses like easy money. And what could be easier than mining the natural forest capital accumulated over centuries in trees and soil—capital in which one invested nothing? Moreover, cumulative ecological damage from overcutting and from excessive removal of downed wood may not show up for decades or more—long after most company executives and most Forest Service administrators are gone. Timber companies therefore have economic incentives to sacrifice the future forest for present dollars by minimizing investment in such stewardship activities as soil improvement, erosion control, and ecological protection. Their sights are instead set on timber market conditions, rates of return on investment, tax code provisions, and ways to operate at least cost and effort. Again, with some noteworthy exceptions, timber companies are generally focused on how the company's profit-and-loss statement will look next quarter, or at most in five to ten years. Against these compelling commercial imperatives are arrayed the dictates of a manager's personal code of behavior, the codes of ethics of the professional societies to which he or she may belong, and the scrutiny of those peers. Often the commercial pressures prevail.

Whereas growing diverse natural forests to biological maturity takes generations, owners meanwhile must care for the land and pay taxes on it. However, the returns on a selectively cut, well-managed forest that is logged on a sustained-yield basis are likely to be only 1 to 2 percent per year of the timber's total cash value. Since that is far less than can be made from a Treasury bond or other competing investment, not many timber companies—even those who claim otherwise—will operate their lands on a sustainable basis, and those public companies that attempt to do so are susceptible to hostile takeovers by more aggressive companies. So it was for the Pacific Lumber Company of northern California, once known for its conservative forestry practices. But after it was bought by the Maxxam Corporation, controlled by financier Charles Hurwitz, Maxxam greatly accelerated its logging on what had been Pacific Lumber's land to raise cash to pay back the loans used for the buyout. Fears of suffering a fate like Pacific Lumber's have driven other timber companies to increase their logging rates in order to better their earnings.

Even growing a commercial crop of trees (as distinct from recreating a forest) may easily take thirty to eighty years, although some construction-grade wood can be grown in only fifteen years. (Wood fiber for pulp, however, may be had far more quickly than dimensional lumber.) Timber prices have to be high indeed for timber investments to compete with earnings that could be had by clearing the land, selling the trees and land, and investing the proceeds to compound for half a century at the prevailing rate of interest.

As author Ray Raphael explains in *Tree Talk,* his tour de force on forestry, "Because of interest computations, economic maturity of the timber occurs long before biological maturity of the trees." This means that trees will be cut before the forest is mature and even before the trees have attained "their maximum annual growth increment"—the point in the tree's life cycle when wood fiber productivity is greatest. Other natural forces tend to push timber companies to hurry trees to market. The sooner the trees can be cut, the less likely that insects, disease, fire, and predation will damage the trees before the timber matures and can be sold. In addition to illustrating the maxim "Haste makes waste," the profit-maximizing, short-rotation, timber-removal cycle disrupts the forest more often than would a longer rotation calibrated to maximize timber volume.

Because of the distant, less certain payoff from reforestation and the more certain, immediate return from logging and selling timber, most commercial timber investment is for expediting logging and other costs of doing business, with only a scant percentage of spending devoted to reforestation and forest management. In addition to all the "perverse incentives" that encourage forest destruction, timber sale conditions and forestry regulations on public forest lands are poorly enforced. Although reforestation, erosion control, and stream corridor protection are mandatory, forests are still routinely badly damaged during logging. Inspections are often inadequate, and potent sanctions for poor performance are lacking or rarely applied.

In *Tree Talk*, Ray Raphael summarizes why timber companies destroy forests: "The whole economic edifice is entirely rational —but it is based on a logic that has nothing at all to do with silviculture." As discussed in Chapter 10, the alternative to "economics first" timber management is sustainable forestry, which legitimizes investment in slowly accruing forest capital.

## Jobs and Forest Protection

While timber companies and their allies like to depict efforts by environmentalists to save ancient forests as the main cause of job losses in the timber industry, this is not the case. Overcutting of timber resources, mechanization of timber harvesting, automation at lumber mills, and the export of raw (unmilled) logs all have a much greater impact on jobs in the timber industry than the campaign to protect old growth.

Regardless of how many board feet are cut today in the Pacific Northwest, employment per board foot cut there has declined by more than a third in the past few years. This has nothing to do with owls and everything to do with technological change in the timber mills. Studies show that, even without environmental restrictions, timber-related jobs in the Douglas fir region of Oregon and Washington will drop by more than half between 1970 and 2000. Conservationists estimate that job losses from automation will cost 25,000 jobs in Washington and Oregon by 2030, three times the loss from reductions in timber harvesting.

Any industry based on a finite diminishing asset, such as old-growth timber, must inevitably run out of raw material and shut down. Timber-dependent communities must adjust to the inevitable and develop economic alternatives. Second-growth timber can be milled where available. Wood products can be manufactured from renewably grown lumber. High-value-added manufacturing, such as furniture making, employs up to twenty-five times more people than logging. Communities have also invested in recreation and ecotourism, and in establishing sustainable forest reserves to provide long-term sources of revenue.

Following a moratorium on old-growth logging in National Forests in Oregon in the early 1990s, timber industry spokesmen tried scare tactics and whipped up the emotions of loggers and others to scapegoat environmentalists. Not only did the economic blackmail fail, but time belied the threats. The state remains a robust timber producer; mills have shifted to smaller timber grown on private tree farms; and many displaced workers are being successfully retrained and are finding skilled work as mechanics, cabinetmakers, and health care personnel. High-technology corporations, such as Sony, continue to be drawn to the state for its attractive quality of life.

Destroying all the old-growth forest would save only a relatively few timber jobs for a few scant years. At that point, the old-growth-dependent jobs would be gone at a gigantic environmental price, and the workers would still be without permanent, sustainable jobs. The sooner the issue of economic conversion and worker retraining is honestly faced, the better local communities will be in the long run by still being able to offer high-quality recreation and an attractive quality of life. The solution is not to destroy the last old tree in the forest, but to assist timber industry workers in finding sustainable jobs. As Alan Durning points out, "Their jobs . . . are no more a reason to continue deforestation than jobs in weapons plants are a reason to go to war."

# CHAPTER 10

# SUSTAINABLE FORESTRY

The essence of a sustainable forest is the ability to
continually harvest the interest without having to touch
the principal.

Craig Blencowe, "Building Up the Forest,"
in *Working Your Woods: An Introductory
Guide to Sustainable Forestry*

Instead of focusing uniquely on commodity timber production, a new movement known as sustainable forestry, begun in the mid-1980s, empha-
sizes protecting the forest's ability to conduct its
natural dynamic processes and functions. As explained earlier,
sustainable forestry means ecological forest management that
maintains a forest's capacity to produce a stable and perpetual
yield of timber and other goods and services. Naturally, this requires providing forest ecosystems with adequate protection
during logging so that they can recuperate fully afterward. All
of the forest's natural resources must be safeguarded, especially
the soil (the forest's basis), the water, any indigenous human
population, the integrity of the forest gene pool, and the survival of the forest's diverse wildlife, even small and seemingly
insignificant creatures, for every living thing naturally found in
the forest has an ecological role that contributes to the forest's
operation.

Because even "good" logging techniques do not invariably avoid the infliction of long-term cumulative damage to the forest, sustainable forestry requires *more* than good technical logging practices; enough of the forest must be left in place after logging so that natural forest processes can continue. If good logging practices do this and protect soil structure, fertility, and forest creatures, then they are probably sustainable. By contrast, using "sustained yield" to refer to forest practices that merely produce a constant annual increment of wood fiber, either in a plantationlike setting or without protecting a forest's natural ecological processes, clearly is misleading. Only one product or crop would be sustained. Other forest outputs and services would be declining or impaired. The forest ecosystem as a whole would be degraded.

Some environmentalists remain skeptical that sustainable forestry is possible. An example of holistic forestry provided by Herb Hammond in his superb book *Seeing the Forest among the Trees* provides strong evidence that it can be done. Hammond tells the story of the 132-acre Wildwood forest near Ladysmith on Vancouver Island. Wildwood had 1.5 million board feet of timber in 1935 and, over a period of a half-century, 1.25 million board feet were removed during nine environmentally sensitive selective loggings that protected old growth, fallen trees, soil, snags, and wildlife. "Today," Hammond reports, "Wildwood is a diverse, intact forest ecosystem with nearly the same volume of standing timber as it had in 1935."

Another example is the Menominee Indians' management of a 200,000-acre forest in Wisconsin. Approximately 1 percent of the forest has been cut annually for the past 140 years, forestry analyst Hans Burkhardt reports in the *International Journal of Ecoforestry* (1996). "This level of harvest," Burkhardt writes, "yields a forest in which lumber is of consistently high quality and quantity, forest inventory is high and non-declining, and associated plant, wildlife and natural systems are flourishing and healthy."

Another example of successful sustainable forestry is the work of forester Craig Blencowe of Fort Bragg, California, documented in *Working Your Woods: An Introductory Guide to Sustainable Forestry,* by the Institute for Sustainable Forestry of Redway, California. In one forest that Blencowe carefully managed over a twenty-five-year period, timber volume tripled, important forest values were protected, a sustained yield of trees was achieved, and more timber was harvested over that time than stood on the land when management began in 1972.

## Good Management and Economic Sustainability

Naturally, if a forester harvests less than the forest's annual growth rate and follows other sound management procedures, the forest's timber volume will inexorably continue increasing until some natural phenomenon brings the increase to a halt by increasing mortality and loss of biomass from the ecosystem. Blencowe (like other sustainable forestry practitioners) manages forests by harvesting less than the growth in forest volume over each harvest cycle until the forest inventory attains a predetermined maximum target volume. He then begins to harvest at regular intervals a volume equal to the forest's growth in the preceding period. This sustainable yield can be cut indefinitely without ever depleting the forest volume below the target level. His goal, however, is also to improve the quality of the working forests that he manages, and maintaining inventory volume does not in itself guarantee maintenance of forest quality. Blencowe therefore uses each of his harvests as a management opportunity "to retain the biggest, best quality and most vigorous trees in the post-harvest inventory to build future inventory." To actualize that management philosophy, he marks inferior and diseased trees for removal (while preserving snags as needed), and he thins suppressed trees to create space for the highest quality trees to be retained. Blencowe is not alone in believing that some of the biggest and best trees of each species should be left in the forest to improve the forest's productivity over time. The sustainable forester's initial emphasis therefore should not be on what to remove from the forest, but on what to leave standing.

With an eye to forest economics, forest ecologist Chris Maser points out, in *Sustainable Forestry: Philosophy, Science, and Economics*, that sustainable forestry is essential not only to the forest but to a sustainable forest products industry, which in turn is a prerequisite for a sustainable society:

> Sustainable forestry is the opposite of plantation management practices today. In plantation management, costs are hidden and deferred to the next rotation or human generation. In sustainable forestry . . . there are no hidden, deferred costs; it is pay-as-you-go forestry that more closely follows Nature's blueprint for maintaining a self-repairing, self-sustaining forest.

To increase the chances of having sustainable forests, ample supplies of dead wood should be left in the forest, along with a sufficient volume of living trees. Downed logs left on the forest floor help restore soil nutrients; dead standing timber provides nesting and roosting habitat for birds; and trees lying across, or lodged within, streams create pools and other needed habitat. Where natural forests are not contiguous due to the effects of prior logging, corridors must be left between forest remnants to permit species to migrate in response to climate change. Minimal but permanent roads help to reduce erosion, according to Maser and others. Damaged areas, especially stream buffers, should be revegetated with native plants, and nonnative species should be removed when possible. Along with an increasing number of forest ecologists, Maser believes that clearcutting and sustainable use are incompatible, and he therefore advocates a permanent end to clearcutting.

## Sustainable Management of Forests: Deciding What Not to Cut

The science of conservation biology provides many useful guidelines that can assist the forest manager in determining what forest stands *not* to cut. Broadly speaking, conservation biology is the interdisciplinary application of biological sciences, especially ecology and genetics, to maximize the survival of natural habitats, ecosystems, and associated biodiversity, along with their natural processes. Several core principles of conservation biology apply not only to the establishment of natural preserves but to the management of natural areas, such as forests.

Two such basic principles are that large preserves are essential to the survival of the most broadly representative biodiversity and that habitat fragmentation inexorably leads to species extinctions. Forest managers thus need to minimize the distance between forest fragments separated by logging so that forest species can commute between otherwise isolated habitat areas and benefit from the resources of the larger area. Similarly, natural forested connective corridors should be left to link "islands" of forest habitat so that species can move freely across whatever is left of their natural range after logging without incurring unnaturally high rates of predation or other risks due to the removal of protective cover and habitat. Corridors should "encompass complete ecosystem types," as Herb Hammond explains in *Seeing the Forest among the Trees,* and should include not only riparian corridors but alpine corridors and "cross valley corridors" that provide a representative assemblage of the local ecosystems along an elevational gradient from valley floor to uplands.

Conservation biology teaches that because of the interdependence of species, predators are essential to the natural functioning of wild forests and other ecosystems. Because large carnivores often require large territories in which to range, forest planners need to take those predators' needs into account when deciding how much forest to spare from logging. Conservation biology draws attention to the unnaturally high rate of species extinction resulting from human disruption of ecosystems. The findings of conservation biology imply that forests containing endangered, threatened, or sensitive species and unique habitats —and particularly those areas rich in biodiversity or essential to the life cycle of a large concentration of a particular species— must be accorded high levels of protection from disturbance in order to protect rarity and shield depleted populations from further stress, as well as to avoid squandering biological abundance where it still exists. Thus, a conscientious forest planner must leave certain areas fully protected. These include old-growth areas and ecologically sensitive zones, such as those with steep, thin soils, as well as high-elevation terrain and riparian zones. Flood plains, wetlands, and riparian zones are of great value to wildlife and are important sources of biodiversity; riparian zones must be off-limits to logging because they are especially erodible, fragile, and hard to revegetate once disrupted.

## Sustainable Management of Previously Cut Forests

Just as restoration forestry (see Chapter 11) is a site-specific art, so sustainable forest management in the context of timber production also must take previous and current site conditions into account. As stated, the sustainable forest manager's general goal must be to maintain all forest processes, structures, and species, as well as to recreate (restore) or perpetuate a naturalistic mature forest. (The word *naturalistic* is used here since forest managers are only mimicking natural processes; their work, by definition, is neither indigenous nor inherently natural to the forest.) In most cases, the naturalistic sustainable forest will also be multi-age and multispecies. (Occasionally, a natural timber stand will happen to be of uniform age, as when a lodgepole pine stand is fully destroyed in a large fire or massive windstorm, and new trees all begin life at about the same time.) To qualify as sustainable, forest management activity must not degrade forest quality over the long term. Rather, it must permit natural forest structure, be it simple or complex, to persist and evolve, thereby retaining most species' habitats.

Whereas various techniques may be adopted to help reproduce a multiage, multispecies naturalistic ecosystem, some enduring principles do apply to all sustainable forestry management. The first principle, as already discussed, is that timber harvest rates must be limited and—on the average—must be less than or equal to the volume of wood produced during the growth cycle between loggings. Local studies of growth and regeneration are necessary to establish the allowable cut. Monitoring subsequently needs to be conducted to verify results over time. Limiting the timber removal rate in this manner precludes the gradual elimination of the forest itself, an inevitable consequence of cutting the forest faster than its natural replenishment rate. With these restraints on timber removal, the forest canopy can be preserved, protecting soil and wildlife and reducing the effect of rainfall on snow, with attendant flooding and soil erosion. Also, with retention of the canopy, forest fragmentation also tends to be minimized.

A second and related sustainability principle is to establish a rotation age for the forest, so that trees are allowed to stand long enough to grow large for their species and to get old enough for the forest to exhibit (and perpetuate) old-growth structure and other conditions. Limiting harvest rates, setting a long rotation period (that mimics natural stand longevity), and managing for structural diversity (a consequence of the multiage, multispecies stand composition) are not only good sustainable forestry practices but serve to preclude large-scale, short-rotation clear-cutting.

At the core of sustainable forest management guidelines are certain proscriptions: Do not simplify the forest ecologically. Do not take more from the forest than the forest can provide and still remain healthy. Do not allow short-term expediency—the desire to minimize management costs and maximize timber production—to reduce the forest's long-term productive capacity. In essence, while gathering some of the forest's bounty, do no intrinsic harm to the forest.

One implication of that dictum is the need to consider the ecological consequences carefully before marking a tree for cutting. The effects of tree removal on illumination of the forest floor and understory trees, for example, needs to be considered. Too little light will suppress tree growth; too much light will produce a short, bushy tree with lots of knots. Logging on fragile soils or in landslide-prone or erosion-prone areas also has to be avoided. A tree can never be uncut, and removing the wrong one can cause enduring ecological damage to a site. Just as the selection of trees for removal requires careful attention, so forester Merv Wilkinson, writing in *Restoration Forestry: An International Guide to Sustainable Forestry Practices*, points out that patient observation is needed to identify trees for retention as "parent trees" for seeding future generations: "A tree needs to be observed over several seasons before it is selected, to see that the cones are abundant, well-developed and not misshapen. Undeveloped cones signal that an aging tree has lost vigor."

Sustainable forest management also requires proper waste

management practices. Burning of slash (organic debris produced during logging) has historically been used as a common
waste disposal technique, often without considering the ecological needs of the forest or the ecological impacts of the fire.
Slash burning is not desirable unless it is consistent with a program of prescribed burns that are beneficial to the forest ecosystem. Although fire occurs naturally in forests and may be prescribed under some management regimes, burning of slash
under conditions likely to produce very hot fires may impair forest recovery. The fire's heat can damage the soil by baking it so
hard that a surface crust forms; even at lower temperatures, fire
can reduce soil fertility by eliminating all litter and humus.

For controlling live vegetation in a sustainable forest management system, manual brush control and mulching are preferable to use of heavy machinery or herbicides. Broadcast spraying of broad-spectrum herbicides should generally be avoided
because of toxicity to beneficial species. Pinpoint applications of
short-lived herbicides by hand painting particular stems is generally considered acceptable, however.

If natural regeneration is occurring, it is generally preferable
to artificial planting of either seeds or seedlings. Natural regeneration tends to be more disease-resistant than artifically planted
stands. When natural regeneration cannot be relied on for some
reason, then seeding with locally adapted native seed is preferable to nonlocal seed, especially to the seeds of genetically en-
gineered "supertrees." These specimens may grow quickly but
are likely to be genetically homogeneous and therefore probably
lack sufficient genetic variability to respond to future climatic
and other stresses. Seeding versus planting seedlings or other
container-grown plants allows for more natural microsite selection and natural root development. Nursery stock may suffer
root deformity or damage if improperly grown or handled and,
even under the best of circumstances, container-grown speci-

mens will experience transplantation shock, which retards development. According to Wilkinson (in *Restoration Forestry*), "A tree that has been transplanted needs eight to ten years to be completely clear of shock."

In keeping with the principle of preserving all essential habitats to maintain biodiversity, sustainable forestry principles include retention of sufficient quantities of snags and downed logs. Just how much to retain is a matter of debate among expert foresters and also varies from ecosystem to ecosystem. But the forest needs some diseased, dying, "defective," and dead trees to maintain all of its ecological functions. While the "defective" tree may, from the mill operator's perspective, be marred by a cavity or peculiar branching structure, it may be perfect for wildlife. Likewise, even when thinning smaller trees, some thickets should be left for wildlife, to mimic the forest's natural variability.

If selective logging of single trees or small groups is adopted, tree removal must be done without construction of an overly extensive road system that causes habitat fragmentation. The downside of removing trees in small groups dispersed throughout otherwise largely unbroken forest is that the resulting edge effects can degrade large areas of the uncut residual forest. Some interior forest species are known to avoid forest areas within 300 feet of sizable clearings. Roads also present barriers to wildlife and serve as veritable thoroughfares for the entry of insect pests, nonnative invasive plants, and fungal diseases.

Selective cuts also must not be performed so as to "high-grade" the forest by removing the biggest and best specimens, leaving only smaller, inferior trees to reproduce. From the vantage point of maximizing long-term forest quality, it makes sense to leave the largest and best specimens standing and remove the worst, working in harmony with natural selection rather than against it. To maintain or encourage the attainment of old-growth characteristics and multiage structural diversity, a restriction on cutting trees larger than a specified breast-height diameter may be made part of the sustainable management plan in some settings for an appropriate period of time, until sufficient numbers of trees reach the desired size.

In selective logging, it is also necessary to avoid too frequent entries into the forest with heavy equipment. The sustainable forester not only wants to manage growth and regeneration, but also seeks to log in the least damaging and least visible ways. To minimize forest damage through soil compaction, for example, horses are generally preferable to tractors for log removal. When machinery is used, it should be the lightest equipment that will do the job. Similarly, rubber-tired vehicles are likely to be less damaging than those with metal treads.

If clearcutting is generally taboo and selective cutting may lead to high-grading and forest fragmentation, what can the sustainable forest manager do? Fortunately, one can avoid the pitfalls of high-grading and fragmentation in selective cutting if trees are properly selected. The strategy should be to focus removal efforts on suppressed (crowded) and inferior trees (culls), on removing excessive fuel loadings, on reducing the density of species made overabundant by fire suppression, and on salvaging damaged or diseased trees while leaving some snags and downed logs. Stands can be thinned to relieve crowding without destroying the forest canopy, and small openings that do not harm forest wildlife can be created by removing trees that are overtopped by a neighbor or that themselves are overtopping potentially more vigorous or superior trees. (If openings are no greater in diameter than the height of the trees, they will mimic the openings created by natural mortality.) A skilled forester can also identify trees that are destined to be shaded out because of their relatively slow growth.

Tree felling can be done carefully with the help of jacks to avoid damaging neighboring trees, and a well-planned skid trail and road system can minimize forest damage during tree removal operations. Road construction should be competently planned and supervised so that road widths are minimized and roads are laid out on well-drained stable soils following natural contours whenever possible, preferably with curves kept to gentle grades.

Although the costs of careful selective tree cutting and removal may be higher than for demolishing a forest in a single clearcutting operation, other management costs are likely to be lower in selective forestry. The healthy, selectively managed forest will not require replanting nor the extensive precommercial thinning operations needed in response to dense regrowth after clearcutting. Nor will it need expensive slash burning and herbicide applications. Because trees under a properly managed canopy will be obliged to "reach for the light," they will tend to grow tall and straight. Under selective sustainable management, a relatively intact forest will also be available for nonconsumptive uses and for the periodic harvesting of a variety of nontimber products. Unlike clearcutting, judicious selective management is consistent with protection of the whole forest—its watershed, its soil, its natural diversity, and the environment. Therefore this management system is truly compatible with multiple use of the forest and with production of a limitless flow of timber into the future. Another virtue of this system is that forest assets appreciate—forest inventory and quality can often be increased for many years before they stabilize—and, so long as the forest is managed sustainably, valuable products can continually be removed to provide owners with steady income and workers with sustainable employment.

## The Controversy over "New Forestry"

A movement known as New Forestry arose in the 1980s out of the frustration some U.S. Forest Service personnel experienced with prevailing management practices in the National Forests. Proponents of New Forestry characterize it as a method of maintaining the forest's physical structure and ecological functions by mimicking the way natural processes, particularly fire, produce disturbance and remove trees, especially in the Pacific Northwest. Various timber management strategies are therefore employed in New Forestry in response to different local conditions and differing interpretations of New Forestry doctrine.

New Forestry theory acknowledges that the entire forest ecosystem is important, that habitats for all species need to be maintained, and that the negative effects of industrial forestry need to be mitigated. Practitioners of New Forestry retain some forest canopy and canopy layers intact and minimize road construction. Buffers of uncut timber are left along watercourses to protect them from siltation and bank erosion. Some trees of each species are left uncut, including some high-quality trees to seed future generations. Prescribed numbers of standing dead and downed timber are also left for wildlife. A site logged according to New Forestry guidelines will therefore be more heterogeneous than a traditional clearcut and will still provide some shade and shelter and exhibit nutrient-cycling processes. But all New Forestry systems are based on clearcutting and even-age forest management. Within that paradigm, New Forestry systems offer techniques for dispersing, shaping, and sizing clearcuts and for blunting their ecological impacts. Yet under one New Forestry management system, as few as eight green trees might be left standing per acre.

As a recent industrial forestry innovation, New Forestry is not universally accepted in the environmental community; its techniques have not been proven through long-term scientific studies; and many forest activists would object to the use of New Forestry techniques on previously roadless areas. Critics of New Forestry see it as an apologia for clearcutting and a screen

behind which to conduct Forest Service "business as usual."
They charge that, whereas the ecological principles espoused by
the scientific founders of New Forestry are laudable, practitioners may be less high-minded and may pay only token heed to
ecosystem values. Some highly qualified forestry experts, however, are extremely enthusiastic about New Forestry and regard
it as a tremendous improvement over traditional industrial forest
practices.

## Forest Certification

Forest certification is a new international movement dedicated to
furthering sustainable forestry by labeling wood and other forest products that have been produced in an environmentally and
socially acceptable manner. A small but growing number of timber producers are seeking certification, and many industrial
users and consumers are showing great interest in obtaining certified products. Some timber wholesalers, such as EcoTimber of
Berkeley, California, buy their wood mostly from certified timber producers. The display of a certification label can thus be a
major advertising and sales boon for participating companies.

To obtain certification, participating forest owners and managers agree to submit to inspections and voluntarily follow forest management practices consistent with standards prescribed
by the certifying organization. The standards are designed to
protect forest functions, processes, habitats, and biodiversity,
and they include a long checklist of do's and don'ts. Among
other things, participating landowners must adopt a forest management plan that balances economic goals with protection of
the forest ecosystem. They must also respect the interests and
welfare of local residents, communities, and workers, and must
protect sites with important cultural significance.

To guarantee that certified forest products are genuine, forest products must be tracked from the forest through shipping, scaling, and milling and on to the marketplace. Because of the potential for abuses and the challenges of enforcing certification globally under widely varying conditions, certifying organizations themselves are accredited by an independent nonprofit group known as the Forest Stewardship Council (FSC). The FSC's label tells consumers that trees and wood products have been produced under environmentally appropriate, socially beneficial, and economically viable forest management. (The FSC was founded in 1993 by diverse stakeholder groups from twenty-five countries; its headquarters are at Avenida Hidalgo 502, Oaxaca, 68000, Mexico.)

In the United States, certification is performed by two entities accredited by the FSC: Scientific Certification Systems (SCS) and the Rainforest Alliance's Smart Wood Program, an international consortium of numerous regional nonprofit forestry groups. In California, for example, Smart Wood certification is conducted by the Institute for Sustainable Forestry, a nonprofit group based in Redway, California. In contrast, SCS is a for-profit entity that has working partnerships with forestry consulting firms around the world.

Beyond evaluating forest management practices, FSC-endorsed certifiers attempt to track the production of wood and other forest products from the forest to the consumer and guarantee that the wood is from a sustainable forest or plantation. All FSC-endorsed certifiers have detailed evaluation criteria that a landowner must satisfy to achieve certification. Following established FSC-protocols, forest practices are examined to ensure their consistency with basic principles of sustainable forestry. (See the accompanying sidebar for an example of one group's sustainability principles.)

# The Ten Elements of Sustainability
## of the Institute for Sustainable Forestry

1. Forest practices will protect, maintain and/or restore the aesthetics, vitality, structure, and functioning of the natural processes, including fire, of the ecosystem and its components at all landscape and time scales.

2. Forest practices will protect, maintain and/or restore surface and groundwater quality and quantity, including aquatic and riparian habitat.

3. Forest practices will protect, maintain and/or restore natural processes of soil fertility, productivity, and stability.

4. Forest practices will protect, maintain and/or restore a natural balance and diversity of native species of the area, including flora, fauna, fungi and microbes, for purposes of the long-term health of ecosystems.

5. Forest practices will encourage a natural regeneration of native species to protect valuable native gene pools.

6. Forest practices will not include the use of artificial chemical fertilizers or synthetic chemical pesticides.

7. Forest practitioners will address the need for local employment and community well-being and will respect workers' rights, including occupational safety, fair compensation, and the right of workers to collectively bargain, and will promote worker-owned and operated organizations.

8. Sites of archaeological, cultural and historical significance will be protected and will receive special consideration.

9. Forest practices executed under a certified Forest Management Plan will be of the appropriate size, scale, time frame, and technology for the parcel, and adopt the appropriate monitoring program, not only in order to avoid negative cumulative impacts, but also to promote beneficial cumulative effects of the forest.

10. Ancient forests will be subject to a moratorium on commercial logging during which time the Institute will participate in research on the ramifications of management in these areas. ❧

*Reprinted by permission of the Institute for Sustainable Forestry.*

## Tree Farms versus Forests

While the sustainability principles outlined in this chapter provide useful guidelines for managers of true forests, some land with trees on it has long since ceased to qualify as forest. How should these areas be regarded? Naturally, tree farms per se are no worse than asparagus fields, citrus groves, or any other kind of farm, all of which produce valuable products and have environmental impacts. But farms should not be confused with forests, and a sustainable yield of farm products should not be confused with proper sustained-yield forestry. Timber companies that claim they are managing timber sustainably but that convert natural old growth or even healthy secondary forests to industrial pulp farms are misrepresenting the facts. Whether the yield is sustainable or not, it is but a single crop, and moreover, the immature timber hurriedly produced from test-tube trees on these farms is not equivalent in strength and density to older, forest-grown timber. Changing a natural hardwood or conifer forest to a more profitable pine or spruce plantation also may have a deleterious affect on soil through the accumulation of more acidic humus. Being more acidic, the litter is more resistant to soil microorganisms and therefore decomposes more slowly. Nutrients in the humus thus become less available for incorporation into the soil and uptake by trees and other plants. All-important soil microflora and invertebrates are likely to be reduced.

Without doubt, original forest values are lost on managed plantations, which seem strangely sterile and are far less interesting places for hiking and wildlife than true, wild forests. The tree farm is also less effective in protecting and purifying water; it is more erosion-prone and has a less complex litter-soil-invertebrate matrix. Finally, nutrient capital is removed wholesale from tree plantations and a sustained yield from farm or forest is impossible if more is taken from them in nutrients and energy than is returned. Perhaps the timber companies engaged in blur-ring the distinctions between tree farms and forests have even deceived themselves with their rhetoric about sustainability. To use a venerable but appropriate cliché, perhaps they have lost sight of the forest for the trees.

# CHAPTER II

# RESTORATION FORESTRY

No big conservation project is adequate in today's
world without a major restoration component. There is
simply too little land left in near-prime condition,
human influences are everywhere, and some ecosystem
types are virtually gone.

Reed F. Noss,
"Wilderness Recovery: Thinking Big
in Restoration Ecology," in *Restoration Forestry*

Restoration means returning an area to an approxi-
mation of its natural baseline conditions prior to a
particular disturbance. In a forest, restoration means
recreating (where absent) naturalistic physical structures, such as a forest canopy and drainage patterns, and natural
properties, such as soil tilth, fertility, and stability, and the
reestablishment of forest processes, such as natural selection, nutrient cycling, and fire, among others. All components of a forest need to be put in good working order or must be on their
way to it, before forest management qualifies as restoration.

Reforestation is entirely different from merely planting trees.
Real forest restoration means attempting to reconstruct an ap-
proximation of the forest ecosystem that existed before logging
or some other disturbance occurred. Thus restoration forestry requires different procedures according to the ecological condi-

tions prevailing in the area to be restored, the site's predisturbance condition, and the manager's goals for the site. If forest damage has been severe and sources of seed in or on the soil are depleted, and no adjacent intact forest exists, restoration may require some reseeding or replanting of ecosystem components, such as shrubs and other understory plants, as well as trees. The reintroduction of absent wildlife and the control of exotic species may also be necessary.

The basic aim of forest restoration is to help the forest heal and return to a state of ecological health in which all natural processes once again function properly, managing the ecosystem and controling its ecological development over time. An important indication of restoration success is the ability to return an ecosystem to a natural, dynamic, self-regulated condition in which a minimum of human intervention is required for ecosystem management. Once forest health and forest processes are restored, the forest will gradually evolve through a sequence of natural developmental changes known as forest succession. In relinquishing control over the ecosystem and returning it to the control of natural processes, the restoration forester must seek to assure that native species can once again reach conditions of normal geographic distributions and abundance and that populations at least be on the path toward normal age distribution. For trees, this means the forest would include young, medium-age, and old trees in approximately natural proportions for the species and site.

Forest restoration also requires the restoration of other ecosystem components, including, for example, natural hydrological regimes. This means restoring surface and groundwater quality and quantity (and timing for surface flows) since these are intrinsic aspects of aquatic systems, which in turn are important components of forest ecosystems. By the same reasoning, the mosaic of other habitats often found in forests, such as meadow, prairie, bog, or fen, may also need to be restored. In short, forest restoration is more than merely re-covering the land with trees.

In addition to seeding, planting, or other revegetation, forest restoration may require a variety of nonhorticultural activities, such as fencing (to protect sensitive riparian zones) or perhaps the removal of fencing and other artificial structures where they are unneeded or harmful to wildlife. Restoration may also require erosion control, road removal or minimization, noxious weed control, and fuel abatement through prescribed burning. Prescribed burning is only one way in which a restorationist initially may need to reintroduce (mimic) natural disturbance regimes. A native plant nursery may also be needed to raise seed and bare root stock for revegetation. Alternatively, wild, locally adapted plant material may need to be collected.

Generally, in North America, the forest ecosystems most likely to engage restorationists' attention are those in which the major recent disturbances have been caused by human intervention—typically road building and logging—following European settlement. Intentional restoration may also be desirable, however, even after some natural catastrophe has destroyed or damaged a forest. Whereas Native Americans altered North American forests over thousands of years with fire and by planting and harvesting edible and useful plants, the interactions between preindustrial indigenous people and forests were in a real sense part of the natural order. Restoration is therefore not intended to return an ecosystem to a condition predating all human contact, even if that were possible.

Types of problems that may require restoration are losses of forest components (trees, shrubs, herbaceous vegetation, litter, snags, downed wood, wildlife, and soil organisms and microbes), loss of soil productivity, loss of native vegetation and invasion by exotic species, loss of species and biological diversity, and erosion and sedimentation of waterways.

Restoration goals, site conditions, and ecological damage considered together by knowledgeable people will suggest the approach and restoration methods to be employed. Restoration requires the specification of attainable restoration goals. The goal may be based on historical information about the forest prior to disturbance, if the information is available, or it may be necessary to use a similar reference area and assume that its characteristics strongly resemble those the damaged forest would exhibit had it not been disturbed.

Forest restoration normally begins with an ecological inventory and assessment in which resources are studied, site conditions are mapped, and ecological damage is described and analyzed. The data gathered in the inventory and assessment phase are used in the establishment of appropriate restoration goals and objectives. The management prescriptions written to achieve these goals and objectives must include not only management practices but the development of a long-term monitoring and assessment plan by which program success can be gauged.

Sites that have been high-graded by selective logging to remove a commercially valuable species from the ecosystem may need to be replanted with local stock of that species (unless the species can regenerate naturally from the seed bank—seeds and propagules already in the soil). Eroding areas, such as stream banks and active landslides, must be mechanically stabilized and planted. Streamsides may need immediate stabilization with logs, rootwads, wattling, erosion control fabric, boulders, and possibly other types of bank armor.

Along with mechanical stabilization, local species found on stream banks prior to disturbance may need to be planted to ensure quicker revegetation under the threat of erosion, or because successful natural revegetation by desired species is unlikely. Whereas fast-growing, short-lived species, such as alder, may provide a quick solution to eroding stream banks (and provide streams with needed inputs of leaf litter), in coniferous forests, long-lived species that grow along waterways may also need to be interplanted along the banks so that, over the long term, the waterways will receive the ecological benefits of large, fallen trees that create pools beneficial to fish.

Actively eroding roads may need to be recontoured, and erosion control devices may need to be installed, repaired, or improved. Unneeded roads should be closed, ripped up with heavy machinery if necessary, and then planted. Other hardened and impermeable compacted soils also may need to be broken up. Trees and other species may need to be reseeded, and where soils are lacking in natural microorganisms, the inoculation of some types of seed with nitrogen-fixing bacteria and mycorrhizal fungi may be advisable to improve plant establishment rates. When the need for ground cover to prevent further erosion is so urgent that it precludes starting plants from seed, shrub and tree seedlings may need to be planted (see Chapter 14).

# CHAPTER 12

# TROPICAL FORESTS AND INTERNATIONAL FORESTRY ISSUES

Among the scenes which are deeply impressed on my
mind, none exceed in sublimity the primeval forests un-
defaced by the hand of man....

Charles Darwin

 Tropical forests are the richest sources of biodiversity in the world, containing two-thirds of
the world's plants on only about 12 percent of its
land area. One forest reserve in Costa Rica has
more plant species than the whole of Great Britain; one river in
Brazil has more fish species than all the rivers of the United
States; one hectare (about 2.5 acres) of Amazon forest may have
forty times the number of species of a typical temperate forest
hectare. A hectare of Atlantic coastal forest in eastern Brazil was
recently found to contain 476 tree species, including 104 never
seen before in that type of forest and 5 previously unknown tree
species (*New York Times,* November 12, 1996). By comparison, a
hectare of North American temperate forest usually has 2 to 20
tree species.

## Tropical Forest Losses

A maelstrom of destruction is engulfing the world's tropical forests—each year, an area about the size of Louisiana is being lost to deforestation in the tropics. Just in a single recent decade (1981–1990), about 385 million acres of tropical forest have been destroyed—an area three times the size of France. During the same period, the amount of sustainably managed forest stayed about the same.

In losing half of its tropical rain forest, the world has also lost thousands of species of life, and is now probably losing more than 130 species a day to extinction, according to the most informed scientific estimates. Without exaggeration, time is rapidly running out for the tropical forests. Only the most courageous, determined, and vigorous sustained efforts offer any hope of stemming the holocaust of forest destruction. The tropical forests are going so fast that less than a third of the countries exporting tropical timber will have anything left to export by the year 2000, according to a World Bank study. Much of the forest that remains has been pillaged for plants and animals and is severely degraded. If current trends in tropical deforestation continue, within about a decade the world will lose all but a few relics of its tropical forests throughout much of their range, much as North America has lost all but 5 to 6 percent of its old-growth forests.

Despite worldwide expressions of concern about tropical rain forest destruction, the continuing and apparently intensifying incineration of the Amazon rain forest region for short-term, low-value agricultural pursuits is a now-classic example of tropical forest mismanagement at its worst. Although the Brazilian government claims that the deforestation has slowed, weather satellite photos revealed more than 72,000 fires burning in the

Amazon just during the first half of August 1995. *As much as 6 million square kilometers (2.3 million square miles) were covered with thick, gray smoke at one time.* Some of the pall hung over Bolivia, Paraguay, and Uruguay as well, indicating that the forest damage is not confined to Brazil. And environmental activists report the impending arrival in the Amazon of some of the world's largest and most rapacious international timber companies, fresh from massive deforestation activities in Asia. Unless their plans are forestalled by a global public outcry and a change of policy by the Brazilian government, these companies and their advanced logging and milling technology will further devastate the Amazon. Whereas the Brazilian government has posed as a friend of the environment and hosted the 1992 Earth Summit, instead of curtailing forest destruction afterward, the government has simply stopped systematically analyzing the crucial satellite image data previously used to monitor the forest's fate.

In addition to uncertainties about the acreages being lost in the Amazon, no one now knows how much of the land being burned is virgin rain forest and how much is second-growth forest and range, nor what the extent of the forest losses are in species and timber, nor what the hydrological cycle and climate stability impacts may be. The Brazilian government reportedly has canceled the subsidies it paid for years to those who cleared the forest, but has apparently allowed the catastrophic conflagrations to continue. Under criticism, Brazil reportedly has now ordered the satellite photo analysis to resume, but it is evidently expressing neither remorse nor commitment to bring the incineration of the Amazon to an end. If Brazil and the world community remain complacent, further massive rain forest despoilment and destruction certainly lie ahead.

In logged and mined tropical forest regions, the lives, lands, and cultures of native peoples have been brutally disrupted.

Even where the forest canopy has not been wrecked, clean forest streams and rivers from which people drank, and in which they bathed and fished, have been turned into muddy, polluted channels, poisoned with mercury and other toxic mining wastes. Much of the fish and wildlife have been driven away or killed. While the indigenous peoples whose homes are being torn apart by forest destruction receive little or no compensation, timber companies reap billions for denuding the forests and destroying species forever: liquidation of tropical forest capital is a lucrative crime.

Forest damage short of total destruction often does not show up in gross statistics of forest loss. The United Nations, for example, does not consider land to be deforested until more than 90 percent of all trees have been cut. Forest fragmentation (separation into isolated units), habitat loss, and therefore biodiversity losses are even more serious than the deforestation statistics suggest. For decades, international organizations, such as the World Bank and the InterAmerican Development Bank, have provided capital for roads, large dams, huge plantations, industrial timber operations, and other projects that have greatly hastened tropical deforestation.

In tropical areas, forests are often completely unable to recover from logging and burning. Tropical rain forest soils tend to be infertile, despite the profusion of vegetation. Most nutrients are found in the standing vegetation, from which they circulate rather rapidly to the soil and back into the vegetational component of the forest. Irreversible soil changes ensue within a few years of exposing many tropical forest soils to the hot sun and torrential rains. The extreme heat of the tropics bakes these soils once trees have been removed and can literally turn the ground into a bricklike material.

In tropical forests, where as much as three-quarters of the

solar energy reaching the forest is used in evapotranspiration (water lost by evaporation from the soil and transpiration by plants), deforestation means that much of the energy will instead heat the air and soil once the trees are gone. Soil temperatures can increase by 9 degrees Fahrenheit locally. Simultaneously, as evapotranspiration is reduced over a large deforested region, the cloud cover will thin, allowing more solar energy to reach the ground. The deforested area will thus become hotter and drier. Other land that depended on the recycling of previously transpired rainfall into new clouds for a cycle of repeated rains will be deprived of the moisture. The reduction in cloud formation will also interfere with the transfer of latent heat from the tropics to the temperate regions. Thus, the effects of large-scale deforestation extend far beyond the former forest land.

The ratio of deforestation to reforestation in the tropics is something like 10 acres to 1. Moreover, little sustainable forestry is being practiced. Rather than experiencing a gradual decline, as do overcut northeastern U.S. forests, species-rich tropical forests are reduced to virtual wastelands within a few years' time. Whole ecosystems and species are being driven to the brink of extinction—or over it—before governments will admit that a crisis exists.

Even if one is unmoved by the horror of destroying exquisite animals and plants for all time, nations that ignore the many utilitarian arguments for tropical forest preservation will pay a steep price. Little-studied tropical forest plants sometimes can be used to improve valuable domestic crops through interbreeding or genetic engineering to increase crop yields or disease resistance. Other plants we are unaware of could be future sources of food, fuel, life-saving medicines, and remarkable scientific knowledge about our own evolution. This alone is sound justification for governmental action.

## Ending Tropical Deforestation: A Complex Challenge

More forceful international environmental leadership by the U.S. government—using the arts of diplomacy, coordinated international efforts, debt forgiveness, and multinational foreign aid—would be invaluable in halting tropical deforestation. All governments must be quickly induced to stop condoning and subsidizing deforestation and to substitute policies and programs that will actively deter it.

Governments can end deforestation both by passing and sternly enforcing protective legislation banning destruction of forests and by using a host of powerful economic weapons. These include ecologically oriented schedules of taxes on conversion of forest land, forest product taxes, forest user fees, and other ecological tariffs to regulate forest use and finance further conservation efforts. Employed in a coordinated program, such taxes, fees, and tariffs can ensure that all ecological costs of deforestation are reflected in forest product prices. This in itself will reduce and rationalize forest product consumption. Finally, where logging is done in spite of conservation efforts, *all timber management plans must be required to meet statuatory tests of sustainability,* and no forest activities that are not sustainable must be permitted.

Because of the speed and pervasiveness with which the world's tropical forests are disappearing, emergency measures are needed on an international scale to confront the problem. In the throes of this global crisis, however, it is easy for well-intentioned people to be misled by simplistic explanations of tropical deforestation and to adopt false solutions. Lasting solutions are complex. It is impossible to disentangle threats to forests from broader threats to the planet's life support systems from multinational corporations, from costly militarism, and from the global processes of industrialization, trade, and rapid population growth.

Some multinationals wield financial resources comparable to those of entire states and nations. They can make huge amounts of capital available for the exploitation of natural resources, even in remote and sparsely developed areas of the world. They exert overwhelming political and economic power on local elected officials, resource agencies, rural communities, and even on national governments, especially in developing nations.

The protection of the world's forests is likewise intertwined with the problems of inequitable distribution of wealth and with the global poverty in which a billion people exist. Whereas the wealthy—especially large landowners—hire others to deforest the tropics for marketable timber, ranches, or agribusiness schemes, many desperately poor people are driven to destroy forests through lack of economic opportunity. More than half of the deforestation in the tropics is done by these "displaced landless peasants." Corrupt politicians are often only too eager to pocket corporate payoffs in return for timber concessions under which forests are legally slaughtered. While the landless, uneducated poor who enter and raze tropical forests in a desperate quest for subsistence can be forgiven because they may have few other options, the tropical forest devastation commissioned by wealthy people out of avarice and indifference to the forest life they are exterminating cannot be excused.

What alternatives do impoverished tropical nations and their people have? Local elites usually are unwilling to act altruistically to save forests by opposing the corporations and individuals destroying them, or by providing capital for local sustainable development projects consistent with forest preservation. Similarly, the amounts of money made available by the national or international community for sustainable development are small. Yet enduring sustainable development requires investment. Some entity must fund not only the creation of nondestructive indigenous industries, but must also provide capital to develop markets for them and to provide the transportation and other infrastructure required to make the new industries economically viable. Many nondestructive multipurpose uses of natural forests can be developed (and are being developed on a small scale), ranging from ecotourism to the gathering of medicinal plants, spices, scents, nuts, latex (for rubber), and fruits. The value of sustainable products like these, collected by local people in a responsible manner, can provide more revenue than either one-time removal of timber or land use for cattle grazing.

Examples of simplistic and misleading explanations of deforestation are that it is caused by overpopulation, by small farmers engaged in shifting cultivation, or primarily to meet the firewood needs of low-income people. These half-truths sometimes lead to blaming the victims of deforestation and turning to its perpetrators for "solutions." True, some 2 billion people in the developing countries depend on wood fuel for cooking, domestic heating, and industrial heat. While this is related, and at times contributes, to deforestation, it by no means adequately explains it. Small-scale village firewood collection should not be confused with deforestation, especially the deforestation that occurs in remote and intact closed-canopy forests. Most firewood collection has been in proximity to population centers, and most villagers gather fallen and dead wood or cut branches rather than chopping down whole trees.

While some wood for domestic use can be grown on managed plantations on previously deforested land, villagers should also have access to affordable and environmentally safe alternative sources of energy. Heat and electricity from a spectrum of solar-based renewable energy sources, for example, could be provided at reasonable cost to peoples of the developing world who have few alternatives to wood. Whereas population density contributes to pressure on land and other natural resources, the impact of population on nature depends on each individual's consumption of energy and other resources (and on the technology being wielded) and on national policies regarding natural resources, not just on the absolute number of people. Inhabitants of affluent industrialized countries have more than forty times the resource impacts of people in developing nations through their greater wealth and per capita energy use.

Instead of helping to solve the problem of deforestation and unsustainable industrial practices, national policy in many tropical nations encourages tropical deforestation. Landless farmers are sent into the forests to colonize them, often displacing forest dwellers. Whereas the landless cultivators are the physical agents of deforestation, however, these impoverished people who do backbreaking labor and often have to live under primitive conditions, "are no more the *cause* of the problem than foot soldiers are the cause of wars" (according to the World Rainforest Movement's *Rainforest Destruction: Causes, Effects and False Solutions*). They have often themselves been displaced from their lands by large, government-sanctioned logging, ranching, farming, and mining schemes, or by large dams. They are both the victims and symptoms of unjust political and social systems. Some governments in the tropics commonly encourage the destructive exploitation of natural resources for the profit of a relatively few government officials and their allies in local and multinational industries. Politicians in developing countries where accountability in public office is not institutionalized may tend to prefer large, expensive "development" projects of all kinds for their country, including deforestation schemes. These megaprojects can bring in large amounts of foreign exchange at once and are particularly vulnerable to graft and corruption. By contrast, small, cost-effective development efforts that benefit large numbers of the poor are usually less attractive to corrupt officials because the flows of money that finance them tend to be less concentrated and are therefore harder to siphon off.

## UNSUCCESSFUL EFFORTS TO REDUCE DEFORESTATION

Reduction of tropical deforestation was the goal of a multibillion-dollar Tropical Forest Action Plan (TFAP), implemented in 1985 by international agencies, including the World Bank, the United Nations Development Programme, and the U.S. Agency for International Development, in cooperation with the World Resources Institute, a U.S. environmental research organization. Under the decade-long management of the United Nations Food and Agriculture Organization, however, the TFAP failed to bring tropical deforestation under control. Other international efforts have also foundered, including the International Tropical Timber Agreement, the International Tropical Timber Organization, and the United Nations Statement of Forest Principles.

The TFAP is a good example of why efforts to halt deforestation have not succeeded. Despite the worldwide dearth of evidence that commercially viable sustained-yield forestry is even possible in tropical forests—and the clear evidence that it is not even attempted when promised—the TFAP was predicated on heavy investments in supposedly sustainable industrial forestry projects. Unlike genuine sustainable forestry, these projects replace natural forests with commercial plantations of eucalyptus and other fast-growing species. Critics of the TFAP pointed out from the start that the plan was not only doomed to failure but would actually exacerbate deforestation, for several reasons. The chief reason is that it does nothing to prevent the large development projects, often funded by the World Bank and other international agencies, which have been responsible for so much tropical deforestation. Instead, the plan treats symptoms rather than underlying causes. In addition, the plan allocates only 10 percent of its budget for protection of intact forest ecosystems (1.5 percent of its budget in Latin America), but proposes billions for investment in industrial forest development. As of 1988, all forty-two of the national plans comprising the TFAP omitted ecosystem restoration, and most ignored multipurpose and traditional uses of natural forests. The rights of indigenous forest dwellers are barely addressed in most of the national plans—a predictable result, given the inadequate and belated involvement of representative grassroots organizations. By contrast, a major pulp and paper company was appointed to draw up the regional forest plan for Nepal and Sri Lanka.

REAL SOLUTIONS

Far greater financial and political commitment must be made to tropical forest protection and to rectifying the fundamental causes of deforestation. These root causes are the unjust and exploitative social, political, and economic conditions that produce and perpetuate concentrated control over land and other resources by elites and multinational corporations. Forest land ownership patterns must be changed in many parts of the world to promote public-interest forest stewardship by well-trained, ecologically qualified forest managers and local traditional forest users. When individuals other than local forest users and public-spirited managers control the forest, disinterest in the forest's welfare and its abuse by excluded users and managers is assured. Often, changing forest land tenure arrangements means empowering indigenous peoples, who have traditionally protected and coexisted with the forest for millennia. But opposition to this is likely from outsiders with greater financial resources and technical skills who are convinced that their "cultural superiority" entitles them to take command of a region's forests and other resources.

Protection of forests also requires repricing forest products to reflect forests' full ecological value—and the full costs of damaging those values. This will be actively resisted by timber producers and consumers. Exploring what the true costs of damaging forests are and how to monetize those costs in a defensible way is a fertile area for economic research. So is investigation into the appropriate amounts to charge forest users (and other beneficiaries) for a broad spectrum of forest-derived benefits. (See Alan Durning's *Saving the Forests* for an interesting discussion of these ideas.) For further discussion of forest subvention payments from developed to developing "forest guardian" nations, see Chapter 13.

The solution to deforestation must include using the "carrot" of development assistance pragmatically to encourage land reform, in conjunction with broader political and economic reform, to achieve more representational government. Even when the international community is unable to encourage socially and environmentally concerned political leadership, it should nonetheless sponsor programs that will make protection of tropical forests financially rewarding to the host nations and their leaders, until more public-spirited political forces can come to power. Billions of dollars need to be made available to compensate developing countries for revenues lost in not destroying their forests, and to physically protect the remaining rain forest. Large sums must also be made available to purchase threatened lands and land development rights, as well as to create and staff forest nature preserves.

Human nature and greed being what they are, fail-safe mechanisms for forest protection must be put in place with international support and bolstered with rigorous enforcement procedures resistant to all manner of continued forest destruction and resource profiteering. Once international funds are available in quantity, they must be used to ensure that ample trained personnel, adequate equipment, and other resources are coordinated by appropriate laws, policies, and unflinching commitment to defend the forests against logging, burning, and unregulated mineral exploitation. Nothing should be allowed to occur that further damages the ecological and hydrological integrity of the forests; disrupts forest dwellers' lives, cultures, or land rights; or reduces biological diversity and the contributions of tropical forests to climate stability.

After the forests have been placed off-limits to industrial development, they should be returned to the native peoples who are most knowledgeable about them and have lived sustainably with them for thousands of years. Granted, some traditional peoples, once in possession of mainstream society's more advanced industrial technology, might be inclined to abandon traditional stewardship practices and liquidate their forest assets for cash. Time and again, local communities, including native residents—either in economic difficulty or tempted by wealth—have sold or damaged their forests. To preclude this, a statutory trust provision may need to be enacted to provide additional protection for repatriated land by attaching an environmental deed restriction to the land prohibiting its deforestation. This might be akin to a conservation easement, a deed restriction on land for which the development rights have been sold and placed in escrow. Regardless of who its custodians may be, threatened tropical forest land must be held inviolate in a perpetual legal trust for humanity and for use in nondestructive traditional ways by native peoples pursuing traditional lifestyles. The application of conservation deed restrictions to the land title, or other appropriate statuatory measures, would then prevent forest destruction by both the original native occupants and any future nontraditional descendants. (Local trusteeship is discussed further in Chapter 13.) By contrast, zoning the forest into nondevelopment and development "sacrifice areas," as some international agencies have suggested, is not going to protect forests in the long term. Similarly, road building into presently inaccessible areas should be stopped, because it opens regions to settlement and is generally the prelude to forest destruction. Intact but accessible areas must be given fail-safe protection.

The international organizations that have funded past destruction of tropical forests should, in reparation, provide funding for the restoration of degraded forest land and the protection of traditional cultures. A portion of these mitigation funds should simultaneously be made available in grants, loans, and debt forgiveness for genuine development efforts in tropical nations to offer impoverished people economic alternatives to deforestation. Such development efforts should always involve indigenous people in program planning and should provide dispossessed and landless people with a means of livelihood on already developed land, as an alternative to forest destruction.

The international aid community is increasing its emphasis on indigenous peoples and is helping to protect some forests in national parks. Innovative programs within the U.S. Agency for International Development have strong linkages with both U.S. and overseas environmental organizations. In addition, a "green seal" program of labeling timber that is produced in environmentally acceptable ways is being developed by the Forest Stewardship Council (see Chapter 10). The new program will create a mechanism for putting consumer pressure on countries that continue destroying their forests. An independent world forestry commission under UN auspices may also be established to further study world deforestation and recommend solutions to the United Nations, which unfortunately lacks the power to enforce them. A renewed commitment to tropical forest conservation was made at the 1992 United Nations Conference on Environment and Development, known as the Earth (or Rio) Summit, and was to have been pursued by the UN Commission on Sustainable Development. Tangible results have been sparse. Neither UN nor other efforts will succeed without an absolute determination to confront the political and economic interests that control forests. While worthwhile, the programs discussed here are but tiny, fragmentary first steps toward the resolution of an immense set of problems that requires a massive, high-priority global effort. On balance, international efforts to date have been misguided and ineffectual, or just too little and too late.

Until the permanent protection of tropical forests is assured, a worldwide ban should be instituted on all imports of timber and wood products from primary tropical forests (in conjunction with other measures noted previously) to communicate a seriousness of purpose to nations with tropical rain forest and to bolster our verbal commitment to forest protection with economic muscle. Imports of beef from deforested areas should be reduced or eliminated to avoid encouraging any further forest removal for ranching. If these measures are ineffective, even more powerful economic sanctions should be implemented. Trade barriers or other economic restrictions would be rescinded as each nation complied with international demands for forest protection.

The alternative to ineffective international forest-saving actions is totally unacceptable: by allowing tropical forests to be exterminated, we will lose as yet undiscovered species and a vast treasure of genetic diversity. Scenes of unimaginable beauty and living resources of inestimable value belonging to all of humanity will be obliterated forever. And more forest dwellers will lose their lives or livelihoods. People who believe that the crime of tropical forest destruction is indeed a high crime against nature and must be brought to an end may wish to work on protecting tropical rain forests through the Rainforest Action Network in San Francisco, the World Rainforest Movement in Penang, Malaysia, or other environmental organizations listed in Appendix A of this book. Only strong pressure from citizens is likely to overcome international complacency about tropical forest destruction.

# CHAPTER 13

# SAVING FORESTS

The world's forest economy functions—or malfunctions
—as it does because its current structure benefits
powerful groups. . . . Overcoming their concentrated
economic and political power will require concerted
campaigns, tireless grassroots organization, and
ingenious political strategies.

Alan Thein Durning,
*Saving the Forests: What Will It Take?*

## Miracles Happen

Against all odds, the vast, lush Kitlope Valley rain
forest of British Columbia, with 800-year-old trees,
fjords, and mountains was saved in 1994 by the voluntary action
of—none other than a timber company. The Kitlope Valley is of
global ecological importance, since it may well be the world's
largest remaining intact coastal temperate rain forest. The 1,224-
square-mile ancient forest has been inhabited for millennia by
the indigenous Haisla nation.

West Fraser Timber Company obtained title to the land from
the government in the 1960s and was preparing to log its timber, worth an estimated $15 million. Although the company
pledged that all the timber work would go to the Haisla, the

Haisla flatly refused to participate and vowed to oppose anything that would harm the valley. Ecotrust of Portland, Oregon, helped the Haisla resist the proposed logging by mapping the Kitlope to document its unique ecological resources. West Fraser Timber then made an honorable and socially responsible decision: it abandoned its logging plans, renounced its title to the Kitlope, and asked for no compensation. British Columbia Premier Mike Harcourt stated that the Kitlope will now be permanently protected. Unfortunately, successes like the Kitlope are all too infrequent, and horror stories of tragic and difficult-to-arrest forest despoliation are all too common, such as the ongoing but little-known destruction of Siberian taiga forests.

## Saving the Siberian Taiga: A Formidable Challenge

The plight of the Siberian forests offers further evidence that it is far easier to propose plausible remedies to deforestation than to implement them politically and economically, or even to alert the world about them. (The account that follows is adapted from work by David Gordon and others at the Siberian Forests Protection Project of the Pacific Environment and Resources Center in Sausalito, California.)

A great deal of damage has already been done to Siberia, not only by recent logging, but by ruthless industrialization during the Soviet era. "Perhaps never has so vast a territory been so despoiled so rapidly," wrote correspondent Eugene Linden from Siberia (*Time*, September 4, 1995). Since the breakup of the Soviet Union and the demise of its strong central government, the economically unstable new regimes that have replaced it are proving receptive to foreign-financed schemes for wholesale exploitation of boreal forest ecosystems, known as taiga. These magnificent, often pristine, swampy coniferous forests extend across Siberia and the Russian Far East. (The moist subarctic spruce and fir forests of Europe and North America are also known as tiaga.) Covering an area the size of the continental United States and twice the size of the Brazilian Amazon, taiga play critical roles in global climate as carbon sinks and sources of oxygen. They also provide sustenance to indigenous hunters, trappers, and fishermen, as well as to endangered Siberian tigers, giant brown bears, sable, and elk. Yet the Siberian taiga is being cut at the rate of 10 million acres a year. When the wood is not exported raw—producing milling jobs and economic activity abroad, instead of in the region—the obsolete and wastefully inefficient Siberian mills consume *three times* the wood for each finished wood product as do modern U.S. mills.

The area bordering the Pechoro-Ilyich Biological Reserve in northern Russia, the largest remaining natural boreal forest in Europe, is now threatened by a huge Western-financed logging concession covering an area half the size of Denmark. Scientists fear that the logging to be done in the reserve's buffer zone will damage the reserve itself and that the soils may not be capable of supporting forest regeneration after clearcutting. Siberian soils are often thin and fragile, and growing seasons are short, making recovery from clearcut logging difficult. In addition, two-thirds of Siberia rests on permafrost, and clearcutting can lead to melting of the permafrost, turning the ground to bog and releasing large quantities of climate-destabilizing methane gas.

Yet 90 percent of Siberian logging is done by clearcutting; environmental assessments are nonexistent; and environmental regulations, such as they are, go largely unenforced. Multinational firms—from Japan, Korea, and elsewhere—that engage in joint ventures with Russian companies are largely unaccountable to citizens for their operations. Japanese companies, which have been responsible for massive tropical deforestation in Malaysia and Indonesia, are now heavily engaged in purchases of boreal forest timber from Siberia, as well as from Alaska and Canada.

Hyundai, the huge Korean conglomerate, has been active since 1990 in the Primorsky region of Siberia. Timber companies have also been eyeing the Botcha River Basin in the Khabarovsk region of the Russian Far East. Unless meaningful international action is taken to ensure protection of the world's last great boreal forests, they will rapidly be destroyed for chopsticks and toilet paper. What strategies, techniques, and tactics offer hope for stemming forest destruction domestically as well as abroad? The balance of this chapter is devoted to consideration of those issues.

## Obstacles to Global Forest Protection

It is easy enough to proclaim that a moratorium should be imposed immediately on destruction of primary tropical forest, ancient old-growth temperate forest, and boreal forest. A moratorium would indeed make sense, ecologically and economically. But major policy decisions about forests are not generally made today on ecological grounds or for the commonweal, but by high government officials "under the influence." The intoxicant, however, is money, not alcohol—and it flows in vast quantities. Corrupt government officials routinely sacrifice forests for personal advancement, to win reelection, or to consolidate power, currying favor with big corporations and betraying public trust in the process. In democracies, timber industry payments may come "above board" as contributions to a politician's campaign coffers; in many Third World tropical nations, payments take the form of outright bribes. In parts of the former Soviet Union, official patronage, favoritism, and corruption are a veritable way of life that is hardly even questioned.

In addition, many honest politicians and government officials throughout the world are simply ignorant of, or oblivious to, intrinsic natural ecological values and services provided by forests and other natural resources. The only values they ascribe to natural resources are those that the resources will bring them on the auction block or in the marketplace. Powerful modern technology and great wealth have empowered them with the means to destroy nature; ecological ignorance and lack of political accountability confer a sense of entitlement to do so. Thus, as nations continue global urbanization and reliance on technologies that enable individuals to separate themselves from and become estranged from nature, political leaders commonly arise capable of sanctioning the destruction of vast ecosystems that sustain us all. Making matters more complicated, all forest sellouts do not occur at the apex of the political pyramid. In some developing countries, in-the-field government forestry officials are so poorly paid that they cannot live on their salaries alone. Unless these forest guardians are paid a decent wage, they will remain susceptible to bribery, selling the forest to help eke out their subsistence.

## Global Forest Protection

Rather than simplistic "quick fixes" to save the world's forests, a comprehensive suite of programs must be put in place to improve the odds of success. These coordinated programs must address the fundamental causes of deforestation and must utilize or amplify those factors protective of forests.

Whereas nothing these days provides forests with ironclad protection, forests tend to be more secure if:

↬ the land is officially recognized to have economic value as a sustainable resource (e.g., for its watershed value); for ecotourism; or for nondestructive cropping of local flora and fauna (medicinal herbs, butterflies, iguanas, etc.)

- ✎ the land is established as an "extractive reserve" on which native people have recognized rights to live and pursue sustainable harvesting of forest products
- ✎ the forests are officially designated as parks, nature reserves, "world heritage sites," or ecotourism destinations
- ✎ property rights of native peoples are recognized and they are made custodians of the land for purposes of sustainable use (minus rights to alienate [sell] the land for development)
- ✎ the forests are clearly demarcated to prevent "accidental" incursions by poachers and timber thieves
- ✎ the forests are culturally regarded as sacred sites
- ✎ the forests are remote from roads and developed areas
- ✎ a professionally trained and properly remunerated cadre of forestry workers safeguards the forest
- ✎ development rights have been "locked up" through the use of conservation easements or other legal means
- ✎ an enforceable legal framework exists for severely punishing abuses of forest regulations

Forest-saving programs thus must be responsive to a whole range of social, spiritual, economic, cultural, historical, and, last but not least, ecological realities.

## Megastrategies for Saving Forests

One basic forest-saving strategy is to ensure that forest protection pays those who safeguard the forests more than forest destruction does. Thus, the road to global forest protection requires that we pay more attention to the trail of money and, even more importantly, to the economics of timber exploitation and protection. Recognizing that economic incentives have to be altered so that it becomes more profitable for governments and people to save forests, rather than to destroy them, a steady stream of payments should be made by nations that can afford to pay—and that benefit from the forests' global services—to forest guardian nations that still have important forests. Payments to developing tropical nations certainly are appropriate in recognition of the tens of billions of dollars (or more) worth of pharmaceuticals that the developed nations have created from compounds that originated in tropical forest plants. Payments to developing nations could also be made to recognize the climate-stabilizing benefits of the forests saved and could represent a form of climate "insurance premium."

Forest guardian nations might also receive money as tacit crop insurance payments for the additional tens of billions of dollars in value that the plant genes of tropical forest plants can save in the future by conferring disease- and pest-resistance on the world's agricultural crops. Payments could be made on a sliding scale and could be contingent on successful action by recipient nations to protect their forests permanently. The better the protection provided, the greater the payments would be. Consistent with the earlier discussion of conservation easements (see Chapter 12), payments could also be construed as easement payments to compensate recipients for not developing forest land and to support them in embarking on programs of nondestructive sustainable forest use.

This subvention strategy admittedly has a serious flaw: it may result in payments to regimes that tyrannize their people as well as destroy their forests. To avoid supporting unjust governments while working for forest protection, parallel efforts need to be made for social justice and in support of democratic leadership. Intense political pressure should accompany offers of tempting aid packages in return for effective forest protection. Another objection to subventions is the risk, perhaps even the probability, that much of the money paid would be misspent or embezzled and that little ultimately may reach the localities where protective actions are needed. While working to create government-to-government subventions for forest protection, forest defenders can simultaneously work to shift control over forests to interest groups most receptive to forest protection and least likely to violate public trust. In practice, this means working to reform patterns of forest property rights, as discussed in Chapter 12. Those groups with the deepest roots in the forest, and therefore the deepest commitment to its protection, are the logical forest stewards and leading candidates for forest trusteeship. But no group, indigenous or other, should be allowed to take actions that destroy the resource base, a common heritage of all peoples.

In conclusion, the aggregate incentives—from the international to the national to the local level—must be orchestrated to reinforce and ensure that forest stewards—be they state forest departments, indigenous peoples, high-level diplomats, businessmen, elected officials, or dictators—all receive far greater rewards for sustainable use of the forest than for destructive, consumptive activities.

## Sanctions for Misdeeds

Concurrent with incentives, *severe penalties need to be put in place for mistreatment of forest land.* These are crimes not only against nature, but against present and future generations, who are being robbed of their natural resource heritage. At a minimum, civil penalties for corporations should include loss of existing timber concessions and loss of the right to contract for future timber purchases. For repeat or flagrant offenders, the response must be suspension or revocation of the right to practice commercial forestry, as well as criminal penalties.

In addition to penalties sufficient to deter malfeasance, stricter enforcement of forest laws and regulations is needed, as well as substantial requirements for bonding, so that ample funds exist to finance attempted restitution of damage, if needed. Funds for more vigorous enforcement of forestry laws and regulations should be derived from "stumpage fees" akin to, but proportionately greater than, royalties paid by mining companies on minerals removed from public lands. In the United States, for example, stumpage fees ought to be sufficient to augment the often inadequate funds available for reforestation through the Knutson-Vandenberg Act. Furthermore, although timber companies logging on the National Forests are already liable for correcting forest damage they cause, these sanctions ought to be much more frequently imposed.

## The Sierra Club's Response to Commercial Logging on U.S. Public Land

In the United States, the Sierra Club has grown frustrated with federal mismanagement of the National Forests and with the resulting forest damage. Since 1996, therefore, the Club has taken a position of outright opposition to any further commercial logging on National Forests or other U.S. public lands. The Club took this stand out of dissatisfaction with consistent failures by the Forest Service and the Bureau of Land Management (BLM) to fulfill their public trust responsibilities. Commercial logging on National Forests and BLM lands has indeed caused severe environmental damage. Wilderness and wildlife habitat have been destroyed and fragmented. Streams have been despoiled. Recreational areas have been obliterated. Millions of acres of land have been ravaged by heavy logging machinery and left in eroded condition, riddled with taxpayer-subsidized logging roads, and otherwise degraded by timber companies while under Forest Service or BLM leases and jurisdiction.

Among the other consequences of commercial logging are substantial flood damage and harm to fishing, recreation, and tourism industries. The two federal agencies have clearly failed to protect public lands from abuse in the past, and the Sierra Club believes them unable to resist timber industry pressure in the future. Moreover, when the dust and logging debris have settled, the havoc wreaked on public lands produces only about 12 percent of the nation's timber supply, an amount easily replaced by recycling of used wood and more efficient wood utilization.

The Club is therefore supporting a bill now pending in Congress called the National Forest Protection Act of 1997, designed to protect and restore the National Forests while providing economic assistance to timber communities. In the preamble to the bill, its authors point out that a majority of Americans think that the National Forests should not be used to produce consumer goods. The bill states, "Ending logging on federal public lands will save taxpayers billions, and help reduce the federal deficit." The bill would prohibit new timber sales on public lands, immediately suspend all sales in old-growth forests and roadless areas, and phase out sales in areas of special ecological significance as well as all other remaining timber sales contracts within two years. (Areas of special ecological significance include late-successional forests, habitat for at-risk species, important watersheds, and wildlife migration routes and corridors.)

The bill would establish a Natural Heritage Restoration Corps in the Department of the Interior to restore commercially logged federal land. Loss of local timber sales receipts would be offset nationally by payments to states for distribution to counties under the Payment in Lieu of Taxes Act (31 U.S.C.s. 6903).

The argument against the Club's position is that ending commercial logging on public lands will merely displace logging to less well regulated private lands, and that much of the public forest already in commercial timber production could now be managed to produce a sustainable timber yield rather than being taken totally out of production. If a natural forest has already

## Alternatives to Trees for Paper Products

The United States currently imports about $4 billion worth of newsprint made from Canadian forests. Yet high-quality paper, cardboard, and fiberboard can be made from other sources of fiber that can be grown sustainably on existing domestic farms. Kenaf and hemp are two practical and renewable alternatives to wood fiber for making paper and paper products. Kenaf, a tall, hardy grass, can produce a smooth, soft, acid-free, chlorine-free paper that is delightful to touch. It also is stronger and whiter, and it yields higher-resolution photo reproductions than newsprint.

Advocates of kenaf claim it can produce five times the pulp per acre as an acre of trees, but at half the cost, while its deep roots remove excess salt from saline soil. Kenaf pulp is also cheaper to process than wood pulp, since kenaf processing requires fewer chemicals and 15 to 25 percent less process energy than the pulping of pines.

Hemp fibers are the longest, strongest, and possibly the most durable alternatives to wood pulp. Hemp is easily grown, widely distributed in northern latitudes, and several times more productive than most tree species, and its processing does not require as much chlorine and other environmentally hazardous chemicals as wood pulp. It can also be grown without pesticides and herbicides. Despite hemp's stigma (because its flowering tops and leaves can be smoked as marijuana), industrial hemp actually contains very little THC, the psychoactive compound in marijuana.

To produce soft paper, hemp may need to be blended with softer fibers, such as kenaf. Although hemp crops may deplete soil nitrogen and require fertilization or rotation with nitrogen-fixing crops, these are far from insurmountable obstacles.

Some Kinko's copy shops already offer hemp paper, and some U.S. paper companies have been seeking permission to grow the fiber domestically. The Greenpeace Catalog and the Real Goods Trading Company of Ukiah, California, both sell kenaf paper. The International Kenaf Association, 101 Depot Street, Ladonia, TX 75449, is a clearinghouse for kenaf information. ✧

been converted to a timber plantation, it might be better to manage it sustainably for timber production rather than to extend timber production onto a natural forest on private land. A forest protection act could accomplish protection of old-growth, roadless, and sensitive areas while still permitting sustainable commercial harvesting of lands that are already de facto tree farms.

## How to Work for Forest Protection

In the United States, citizens can help protect forest resources in many ways—from commenting incisively on a proposed Forest Service timber sale (see Chapter 5), to planting a grove of trees or shelter belt (see Chapter 14), to helping to save and restore a large forest (see Chapter 11). Other ways of saving forests include reducing our consumption of forest products: since much of the forest destruction in the world is driven by demand for pulp, paper, timber, and other wood products, the more we personally conserve, recycle, and avoid unnecessary packaging, the less we contribute to deforestation. (See sidebars "Demand for Wood *Can* Be Reduced" and "Alternatives to Trees for Paper Products.") We can also work in many ways in the political arena, at the county, state, federal, and international level, or by participating in direct action and civil disobedience. The important thing is to take *some* forest-saving action. Even if those actions seem small relative to the challenge, they may inspire others and lead to important and sometimes unforeseeable results. As we continue learning about forest and wildlife issues, for example, we can share our growing knowledge with friends, coworkers, neighbors, and children. A child taught to love and respect nature today may be tomorrow's John Muir or Rachel Carson.

There are countless paths for sharing knowledge and communicating our concerns—from organizing concerned citizens to campaign for a wilderness area, to protecting an old-growth grove targeted for logging, to planting trees in a greenbelt, to helping park personnel restore damaged public forests, to urging timber and paper companies whose stock one may own to manage their commercial forests sustainably, to urging lumber retailers not to carry old-growth wood or lumber from forests not sustainably managed. From writing an influential letter to the

## Demand for Wood *Can* Be Reduced

The nations of the world have enormous opportunities for reducing wood consumption, recycling wood pulp, and substituting other sources of pulp for trees. All the wood fiber that has already been processed or that is already being farmed must be utilized efficiently before we dream of further damaging forests of high ecological value. According to the Worldwatch Institute, **one of every two trees cut is wasted through inefficient wood utilitzation and failure to recycle.**

Globally, more than half of all wood used is consumed as fuel. But as countries urbanize and industrialize, they can increase the efficiency of wood processing and combustion and can also substitute other fuels for wood. Wood consumption can therefore diminish, just as it has in industrialized nations for the past century.

In addition to the available alternatives to trees for paper goods, excellent alternatives to trees for construction materials exist. For example, nonwood fibers can be incorporated into pressed-board products for which solid board was once needed. This suggests that by using environmentally preferable substitutes and simultaneously raising the cost of solid wood through public policies, conservation and greater efficiency in wood use could eventually lower wood consumption, provided that population growth does not outpace conservation efforts. For more information on substitutes for wood, see "Shopper, Spare that Tree," by Vince Bielski, in the July/August 1996 issue of *Sierra*; for alternatives to tropical wood, contact the Rainforest Action Network for copies of their fact sheets on these topics.

editor, to lobbying for a bill to stop all commercial logging on public lands, to drafting legislation, providing critical testimony, circulating petitions, or writing newspaper and magazine articles that call attention to threatened forest resources. From convincing developers, local businesses, and utilities to plant native trees to coordinating native tree planting projects with local schoolchildren, neighborhood people, and local native plant nurseries.

In embarking on forest protection or environmental work of any kind, remember Catholic Worker Amon Hennessey's admonition: Never underestimate the power of the committed individual to act effectively for good. Especially if one perseveres and joins together with like-minded people, the work could lead to the protection of a threatened wilderness or to the creation of a forest park, wildlife refuge, or national monument. It is so easy to be politically passive, complacent, and uninvolved in determining the outcome of today's critical environmental and political crises. But it is deeply rewarding to have an influence on problems far beyond what may seem possible.

Conservation leader extraordinaire David Brower once said, "How many people was Rachel Carson?" One could also ask, "How many people is David Brower, Sierra Club board member and former executive director, founder of both Friends of the Earth and of Earth Island Institute, and a powerful force behind myriad conservation victories? Or how many is the Sierra Club's Dr. Edgar Wayburn, who campaigned successfully for the protection of 100 million acres of Alaskan public lands? Or Earth First! cofounder Dave Foreman, who again and again placed himself in front of loggers bent on old-growth destruction, and whose passionate speech, deeds, and writing have awakened millions of Americans to the perils threatening their forests, wilderness, and wildlife? How many people, too, was John Muir, who founded the Sierra Club, led the successful campaign for Yosemite National Park, and helped inspire Theodore Roosevelt to establish wilderness reserves, national monuments, and parks? Finally, how many people was Dr. Richard St. Barbe Baker, who during his life initiated programs that led to the planting of 26 *billion* trees?

Trite as it sounds, it is absolutely essential to let your state legislators, forestry board, governor, congressional representatives, president, and cabinet members know that you support protection of all old-growth forest, parks, and wilderness. Write, call, and visit these people, who have the power to save endangered ecosystems and species and who control funds that could mitigate damage to them. *Develop long-term relationships with these leaders.* They may gradually come to respect your knowledge, concern, and perseverance in working to improve natural resources management. Let the media know of important environmental issues that concern you by calling, writing, and meeting with members of the press.

Finally, work together with environmental organizations and grassroots groups (see Appendix A) to protect and expand designated wilderness, parks, and ecosystem restoration efforts. The National Wildlife Federation's *Conservation Directory* can acquaint you with the broad spectrum of groups employing a wide range of conservation tactics—from court action to public education to land trust formation to direct action. The Ecology Center of Southern California also publishes a very comprehensive environmental group directory. These groups will invariably be eager to tell you about their work and invite your participation and support. For additional forest-saving ideas, consult the forestry sections of *This Land Is Your Land* or *Design for a Livable Planet*, or see *Saving the Forests: What Will It Take?*, *Saving Our Ancient Forests, Who Will Save the Forests?* and *Saving Nature's Legacy*, all listed in Recommended Reading at the back of this book.

One last note: for inspiration regarding grassroots forest-saving action, remember the Chipko ("hug a tree") movement, perhaps the world's most famous grassroots ecological campaign. The movement began in 1973 among the peasants of the Himalayan foothill country of Uttarakhand, in Uttar Pradesh, India, situated between Nepal and Kashmir. Women played a prominent role in Chipko, but it was a broad social movement supported by men and children as well. The women of Uttarakhand hugged trees in nonviolent resistance to the state and private logging contractors who tried to cut down the local forests. Chipko's successful direct actions not only led to a moratorium on the felling of live trees in Uttarakhand, but inspired other forest defenders in India and around the world, including the grassroots, direct-action forest protection movement in the United States, epitomized by Earth First! Through its reforestation work, marches, and other activities, Chipko expressed an inherently powerful vision of an ecologically sustainable and economically just society. (For a detailed account of the Chipko movement, see *Who Will Save the Forests?*)

# CHAPTER 14

# HOW TO PLANT TREES

Work with nature! Invariably "nature knows best. . . ."

Merv Wilkinson,
"Wildwood, A Forest for the Future,"
in *Restoration Forestry*

As the chapter on forest restoration makes clear, planting a tree—or any isolated component of a forest, for that matter—is not in itself forest restoration, contrary to what decades of forest industry misinformation has led many Americans to believe. Why, then, include a chapter on tree planting here? Because under certain conditions, where natural regeneration has faltered, tree planting may be a beneficial or necessary phase in a forest recovery program. And tree planting in currently treeless areas where trees have historically been found, or in ecologically damaged areas, such as eroding hillsides or mined lands, can be of great benefit to the air, soil, water, and wildlife, even if the trees are small in number, lack supporting forest integuments, and for other reasons do not reconstitute a viable forest.

Despite these reasons, some dedicated environmentalists understandably still regard tree planting as a feel-good diversion likely to detract attention from forest protection or from fundamental causes of environmental disruption. But before accepting that assessment and dismissing the value of tree planting, let's not forget that while planting a single tree may seem like a small gesture, this simple act can be multiplied millions and even billions of times with enough public support until significant local and regional ecological benefits are realized. These benefits can include soil protection, flood prevention, wildlife habitat, aesthetic rewards, production of fruits, nuts, fiber, building materials, and useful renewable fuels, and airborne carbon dioxide removal. Tree planting can also modulate local temperature extremes. In lowering peak summer air temperatures in urban areas that become hotter than their surroundings, air-conditioning energy can be saved and significant reductions in smog can be achieved, since smog formation is temperature sensitive. These effects have been documented in studies by Dr. Arthur Rosenfeld and others at the Lawrence Berkeley National Laboratory.

## The Basics of Tree Planting

Apart from all the social and environmental benefits, planting a tree is a joyful activity and, fortunately, it's also easy. All you need is to keep in mind the basic things that a tree requires: sunlight, water, carbon dioxide, oxygen, and space in which to grow, plus micro- and macronutrients. A tree may also need shade, protection from wind, and the presence of beneficial organisms to make soil nutrients more available and to assist in seed dispersal and germination.

If you are attempting to plant a forest or woodland with native species rather than a tree or two, first convince yourself that properly protected natural regeneration will not accomplish the job. Sometimes fencing an area to protect it from livestock or human foot traffic may be all that is needed for its natural recovery. If planting is necessary, try to use locally grown and therefore locally adapted seed or plant stock. Even trees of the same species grown elsewhere in the region may not do as well in your particular soil and microclimate as trees whose ancestors have been there adapting to local conditions for thousands of years or more. If you are choosing to grow nonnative species for ornamental purposes, consider whether the reasons for using nonnatives outweigh the environmental benefits of restoring native vegetation, to which local native animal and plant species are adapted.

While seeds are less expensive than seedlings, their survival is less certain. The smaller and younger the sprout, the more vulnerable it is to drought, shading, sunscald, and other physical damage. Seeds are also susceptible to wildlife predation. Extra seed is normally planted in expectation of inevitable losses. (They can be coated with repellent or fungicide to minimize losses.) To improve plant survival on inhospitable sites or where livestock or wildlife predation is expected, seedlings may benefit from extra help, including bud capping and caging (to protect against browsing), screening and shading to protect against full sun, mulching to help deter competing weedy vegetation, fertilization to compensate for soil deficiencies, and watering or irrigation to aid plant establishment.

Successful planting begins with the selection of healthy, undamaged, and pest-free stock. If using container stock, make sure the roots are neither circling nor kinked. Check this by exposing about an inch of soil with your finger. When planting, think about how the mature trees will fit into their environment. Make sure that they will not interfere with each other. If attempting to simulate a forest, space the trees irregularly rather than on a uniform grid and allow for some forest openings. Most trees should be 6 or 8 feet apart. If planting seedlings, allow for average seedling mortality, which is usually at least 25 percent. (Some experts put it as high as 40 percent.) Naturally, plant seedlings or trees that have spreading foliage farther apart than those that are more upright in form. Try to include the native understory plants if these are missing from the ecosystem, particularly species with edible seed pods, fruits, and nuts to support wildlife.

The forest stand or other planting area will probably have significant variations in slope, aspect, exposure, soil, and competing vegetation. The combined effect of these variables creates different "microsites." Some will be cooler or warmer, windier or calmer, foggier on the coast side of a mountain or drier toward the interior. Match planting sites as closely as possible to your trees' requirements. If planting on a hill, consider whether the slope has southern or northern exposure. Some trees are more shade tolerant and may do well in the shelter of a bluff or if partially shaded by existing forest canopy. Other species like full sun or only some direct sun. Similarly, some trees will flourish in poorly drained soils, whereas other drought-tolerant trees require the substrate to be well drained and can be planted in sandy soils.

To maximize the chances of seedlings' or seeds' survival, competing brush, grasses, and weeds must be removed around the new plantings. Sites can be cleared manually with heavy brush cutting and grubbing tools, such as a pulaski (a pick and ax combination), hoes, mattocks (a pick and hoe combination), shovels, chainsaws, and Brush Kings (gas-driven circular saws). On a large site, or one that is overgrown with heavy brush, site preparation can be done by controlled burning or heavy machinery, such as a bulldozer or tractor dragging brush rakes, harrows, or discs, to prepare the ground. (Controlled burning requires a permit, so check with your local fire department.) Light brush can usually be pushed aside into piles manually, or by a bulldozer if necessary, along with debris and logging slash.

Other control methods include the use of short-acting herbicides applied directly to stems or small areas and intense browsing and grazing by livestock. Professional advice and assistance should be obtained for all but manual brush-clearing methods. Mechanical seedling planters also exist, but seedling survival is generally higher with hand planting.

Generally, planting should be done in late fall or early spring. Hand planting techniques differ, depending on the seedling's size. Planting a small seedling from a tube with its plug of earth generally requires only a couple of deft strokes with a short hoe, planting bar, or shovel. Technique depends on tool choice and site conditions. (Any of two dozen tools may be used.) When a spade or shovel is used, a hole is dug and the seedling is inserted perpendicular to the horizontal plane of the soil, regardless of the ground's slope. For proper tree growth, roots must have enough room to hang straight down in the hole and must not be either jammed together, bent into a J, or forced to circle the hole. Seedlings do not need to be staked. The roots of a bare root seedling should be pruned to remove dead or damaged roots and then soaked overnight in water before planting. Avoid exposing roots to air, because tiny roots will dry out immediately, and the tree will be harmed.

If it's a conifer, the tree should be covered with soil to just below the start of the needles. Deciduous trees should be planted with the top of their root crown flush with the soil level. Planting lower leads to root crown rot, and planting higher causes drying. A timed-release fertilizer tab may be inserted in the bottom of the hole to aid the tree in getting established. If the terrain is rocky, trees can even be planted among rocks, provided that the hole is filled with soil and that water can drain around the rocks. If the soil is very compacted, it may be necessary to auger or dig it out and then backfill the soil into the hole, making it easier for the tree to get established. For further details on planting and caring for forests, see James R. Fazio's *The Woodland Steward*. Information on yard and ornamental trees can be obtained from gardening books, such as those published by Sunset.

Once the tree is planted, the hole is refilled with soil, which is tamped down around the seedling with the heel of the planter's boot or shoe to eliminate air pockets. When a planting bar, hoe, or mattock is used, the procedure is similar, but the tool is inserted into the soil near the first hole or slit into which the seedling has been placed and is then used as a lever to force the soil to close on the hole, compressing the soil firmly around the roots. The second hole is also filled to prevent drying of the nearby seedling's roots. Finally, the soil is packed down around the seedling with the heel of the planter's boot.

If planting a well-developed tree with soil from a pot or in a rootball, the hole needs to be correctly sized, and care must be taken to ensure adequate contact between the rootball with its soil and the surrounding ground so that the roots do not dry out. Container-grown trees should have a temporary watering basin—a circular rim of earth built around the tree well beyond the circle formed by its outermost branches—to hold water in this area and thus increase water percolation to the roots.

If the tree comes in a large container with a heavy mass of soil around its roots, tap the container to loosen the mass, tilt the container, and slide the tree out onto a shovel or the ground to support the tree. Lifting the tree and root mass by its trunk can damage the roots. Some experts advise gently spraying away the outer inch or so of soil from around the roots with a garden hose. Staking is not recommended unless the tree is unable to support itself. When the hole is prepared, tamp soil down in the bottom firmly enough so that the tree will not settle, but not so tightly that the packed soil forms a barrier for the roots. If the sides of the hole are smooth, roughen them to facilitate root penetration. (Use a spade to continue supporting the tree as you set it into the hole.) Once the tree is in the hole, check to see that the top of the root mass is flush with the ground surface.

As with seedlings, any roots left exposed to the air can become dry and damaged, whereas piling soil against the trunk can lead to rot. However, in a hot, arid area with sandy soil and occasional wet winters, it may be preferable to plant the tree lower in the ground to avoid drying the root collar. In some climates, natural rainfall may be sufficient to establish new trees with a high probability of success. Otherwise, the trees may require irrigation or individual, deep watering in the dry season until their roots reach the damp soil of the water table or become hardy enough to depend on the vagaries of natural rainfall. Two or three growing seasons (or more) may be required until this occurs, depending on ground conditions. The frequency of watering depends on climate, species, and soil. The rule is that the root zone should be moist but well drained. You may need to water as often as once a week (or more) for the first two or three years during the dry season to keep roots moist. Monthly watering (or none) may be sufficient during the third dry season. Excessive watering that causes a tree to remain wet is likely to cause fungus.

After planting, stands of trees will benefit from weeding, brush control, thinning, improvement cutting (to remove defective trees), and pruning. Protection from uncontrolled and unwanted fire, insects, damage, and disease may also be necessary. Finally, unless your silvicultural goal is forest preservation, you will need to know when and how to harvest commercial timber. All these subjects are well introduced in *The Woodland Steward*, cited earlier. Specific advice about particular trees in your area can be obtained from local nurseries, federal and state agricultural agencies, forestry departments, the library, and foresters at colleges and universities. The general growing requirements for each tree species may be found in a botanical encyclopedia.

## Welcome Mats for Wildlife

If you're lucky enough to have property where trees will grow, you can also have lots of fun by managing the land for native wildlife. By observing your land carefully and thinking like the wildlife you wish to attract, you can often determine what it lacks in the way of food, water, or shelter. If any of these ingredients are in short supply, providing them will improve the carrying capacity of the habitat. Nesting cavities, dens, brush piles, hedgerows, and ditches all have their functions as shelter for wildlife. Many species can benefit from nut trees, such as oaks, hickories, walnuts, and pinyon pines, as food sources. Wildlife also appreciate autumn olive, cherry, crabapple and apple, American cranberry bush, and holly. If desirable, small springs and seeps can be developed into more accessible water sources, ponds can be created or expanded, and catchments can be built where rainwater is scarce.

Books on wildlife management, local fish and game officers, soil conservation district agents, or wildlife management professors can be sources of additional ideas suitable for your land. Two excellent introductory books are Malcolm Margolin's *The Earth Manual: How to Work on Wild Land Without Taming It* and James R. Fazio's *The Woodland Steward*.

Although you'll be mopping the sweat from your brow when tree planting, you can dream of how wonderful your forest will be once your seedlings or saplings reach maturity. Imagine what the spot will look like with mighty trees reaching a hundred feet into the sky. Children may play beneath them in the cool shade. One day hundreds of years from now, the trees may become old growth. You can take satisfaction now in the joy these trees will give people generations from now and the good that the trees will do meanwhile for the living Earth. Perhaps you will also draw strength and confidence from these simple good deeds to work in other ways, politically and educationally, for healthy, sustainable forests.

# ENVIRONMENTAL ORGANIZATIONS

*Adapted and updated with permission from* This Land Is Your Land, *by Jon Naar and Alex Naar (HarperCollins, 1993).*

## North American Organizations

ALASKA CONSERVATION
  FOUNDATION
750 West Second Avenue, #104
Anchorage, AK 99501-2167
(907) 276-1917

ALLIANCE FOR THE WILD
  ROCKIES
P.O. Box 8731
Missoula, MT 59807
(406) 721-5420

AMERICAN WILDLANDS
6551 S. Revere Parkway, #160
Englewood, CO 80111
(303) 649-1211;
fax (303) 649-1221

ASSOCIATION OF FOREST
  SERVICE EMPLOYEES FOR
  ENVIRONMENTAL ETHICS
P.O. Box 11615
Eugene, OR 97440
(503) 484-2692

DEFENDERS OF WILDLIFE
1101 Fourteenth Street, NW,
Suite 1400
Washington, DC 20005
(202) 682-9400;
fax (202) 682-2309

EARTH FIRST JOURNAL
P.O. Box 1415
Eugene, OR 97440
(503) 741-9191

EARTH ISLAND INSTITUTE
300 Broadway, Suite 28
San Francisco, CA 94133
(415) 788-3666

ENVIRONMENTAL ACTION, INC.
6930 Carroll Avenue, Suite 600
Takoma Park, MD 20912
(301) 891-1100

FOREST GUARDIANS
612 Old Santa Fe Trail, Suite B
Santa Fe, NM 87501
(505) 988-9126

FRIENDS OF THE EARTH, INC.
1025 Vermont Ave., NW, #300
Washington, DC 20005
(202) 783-7400

GLOBAL ReLEAF
American Forests
P.O. Box 2000
Washington, DC 20013
(202) 667-3300

GREATER ECOSYSTEM
ALLIANCE
P.O. Box 2813
Bellingham, WA 98227
(360) 671-9950

GREATER YELLOWSTONE
COALITION
P.O. Box 1874
Bozeman, MT 59771
(406) 586-1593

GREENPEACE USA
1436 U Street, NW
Washington, DC 20009
(202) 462-1177

LAND TRUST ALLIANCE
1319 F Street, NW, Suite 501
Washington, DC 20004-1100
(202) 638-4725

LIGHTHAWK
P.O. Box 8163
Santa Fe, NM 87504-8163
(505) 982-9656

NATIONAL AUDUBON SOCIETY
1901 Pennsylvania Avenue, NW,
Suite 1100
Washington, DC 20006
(202) 861-2242

NATIONAL WILDLIFE
FEDERATION
1400 Sixteenth Street, NW
Washington, DC 20036
(202) 797-6800

NATIVE FOREST COUNCIL
P.O. Box 2171
Eugene, OR 97402
(503) 688-2600

NATURAL RESOURCES
DEFENSE COUNCIL
40 West Twentieth Street
New York, NY 10011
(212) 727-2700

THE NATURE CONSERVANCY
1815 North Lynn Street
Arlington, VA 22209
(703) 841-5300

PACIFIC ENVIRONMENT &
RESOURCES CENTER
Fort Cronkhite, Building 1055
Sausalito, CA 94965
(415) 332-8200

PUBLIC FORESTRY
FOUNDATION
P.O. Box 371
Eugene, OR 97440-0371
(503) 687-1993 (fax same)

RAINFOREST ACTION
NETWORK
450 Sansome Street, Suite 70
San Francisco, CA 94111
(415) 398-4404

RAINFOREST ALLIANCE
65 Bleeker Street
New York, NY 10012-2420
(212) 677-1900

SAVE AMERICA'S FORESTS
4 Library Court, SE
Washington, DC 20003
(202) 544-9219

SAVE-THE-REDWOODS LEAGUE
114 Sansome Street, Room 605
San Francisco, CA 94104
(415) 362-2352

SIERRA CLUB
85 Second Street, Second Floor
San Francisco, CA 94105-3441
(415) 977-5500

SIERRA MADRE PROJECT
P.O. Box 41416
Tucson, AZ 85717-1416
(520) 326-2511

SOUTHEAST ALASKA CONSER-
VATION COUNCIL
419 Sixth Street, #328
Juneau, AK 99801
(907) 586-6942

TREEPEOPLE
12601 Mulholland Drive
Beverly Hills, CA 90210
(818) 753-4600

WILDERNESS SOCIETY
900 Seventeenth Street, NW
Washington, DC 20006
(202) 833-2300

WILDLIFE CONSERVATION
INTERNATIONAL NEW YORK
ZOOLOGICAL SOCIETY
185th Street and Southern
Boulevard, Building A
Bronx, NY 10460
(718) 220-5100

WORLD WILDLIFE FUND–US
1250 Twenty-fourth Street, NW
Washington, DC 20037
(202) 293-4800

WORLDWATCH INSTITUTE
1776 Massachusetts Avenue, NW
Washington, DC 20036
(202) 452-1999

## International Organizations

TAIGA RESCUE NETWORK
Ajtte, Box 116, S-962 23
Jokkmokk, Sweden
Telephone: 46-971-17037;
fax: 46-971-12057;
e-mail: kldahl@pns.apc.org

WORLD RAINFOREST
  MOVEMENT
Attn: Martin Khor Kok, Third
World Network
87 Cantonment Road
Penang, Malaysia

For additional listings of international forest-protection organizations, see *Restoration Forestry,* edited by Michael Pilarski, in "Recommended Reading."

# GLOSSARY

**autotroph** Literally, "self-feeder." A class of organism, including all green plants, certain bacteria, and certain protozoa, capable of synthesizing organic nutrients from carbon dioxide or carbonates and inorganic nitrogen using energy obtained from light rather than by consuming plants or other autotrophs. (Also, certain bacteria that obtain their energy from sulfur-containing compounds rather than from solar energy or from other autotrophs.)

**board foot** The volume of a board that is a foot in length, a foot in width, and an inch in height, thus 144 cubic inches.

**boreal** Of or pertaining to the northern terrestrial biogeographic zone of the Northern Hemisphere, characterized biotically by the dominance of coniferous forests and tundra.

**clearcut** A former forest or timbered site on which all the trees have been cut down.

**coniferous** Pertaining to trees or to an area dominated by trees of the order Pinales that bear cones, such as pine, fir, spruce, cypress, yew, and redwood.

**controlled burn** An intentionally set and contained fire in a forest or stand of trees ignited for the purpose of improving the area's ecological health or condition—for example, by reducing the accumulation of flammable material or by controlling pests, pathogens, or invasive species.

**deciduous** Dropping or shedding leaves on an annual basis at the end of the growing season.

**detritus** Loose, fragmentary material found on the forest floor, derived from the breakup of rock or organic material, or found on the bed of an aquatic system, including dead leaves, twigs, and decaying and excreted matter.

**epiphyte** A nonparasitic plant that grows on another plant or inanimate structure and gets its nutrients and moisture from the air.

**evapotranspiration** The loss of water resulting from a combination of evaporation from soil and water surfaces, plant surfaces, and plant transpiration (the removal of water from soil by plants and its subsequent release as water vapor to the atmosphere).

**evergreen** Nondeciduous; having foliage that is perennially green.

**food web** The network of organisms that supply and consume food (nutrients and energy) in an ecosystem. In a simpler, linear component of a food web known as a food chain, the organisms that are lower on the chain (closer to the autotrophs at its base) supply food to those higher up. Also sometimes called a food pyramid.

**forest management plan** A strategic document outlining management goals, objectives, and practices for a forest.

**heterogeneity** The state or quality of being heterogeneous—that is, having a dissimilar, irregular, or otherwise diverse nature, components, or ingredients. A heterogeneous habitat thus provides a large range of ecological niches (see *niche*).

**heterotroph** An organism that feeds upon autotrophs because it is unable to combine carbon dioxide or carbonates with inorganic nitrogen to produce its own complex organic compounds.

**industrial forest** A forest that is harvested annually and owned by a company that has wood-processing capacity and a full-time forestry staff.

**integrated pest management** (IPM) A sophisticated system of controlling forest diseases and pests through a combination of applied ecology (e.g., the use of natural predators, elimination of alternate hosts, modified cutting) and strategic applications of pesticide based on knowledge of pest life cycles and population dynamics in order to achieve pest control with a minimum amount of pesticide.

**microclimate** The highly variable meteorological conditions found on different small parts of a site because of local geophysical features that produce variations in moisture, shading, temperature, and sheltering.

**microsite** A specific small location on a tract of land with a set of distinctive ecological conditions favorable to certain organisms with regard to moisture, soil, exposure, and illumination.

**monoculture** The cultivation of a single species of plant to the exclusion of other species.

**montane** Of or pertaining to the biogeographic zone of cool, moist, mountain slopes below timberline dominated by large conifers and associated plants.

**mycelium** A mass of interwoven hyphae (filaments) produced by a fungus (and some bacteria) and penetrating the host or substrate to which the fungus is attached.

**mycorrhizae** Soil fungi that grow on decaying matter and are symbiotically in contact with the roots of certain trees and other vegetation, exchanging inorganic nutrients (mainly phosphorus) with those roots in return for sugars and other compounds.

**niche** A particular type of physical locale providing the specific conditions required for a particular organism; also the particular role that an organism or taxon fulfills in its ecosystem, as indicated by its activities and resource use.

**old growth** Mature, generally large, old trees and their associated natural conditions relatively uninfluenced by post-industrial age human activities. Forest old growth, as opposed to a stand of trees, is structurally complex, with wide varitions in tree size and age. See pp. 22–24.

**patch cut** A clearcut of relatively small size surrounded by uncut forest or stands.

**percolation** The infiltration of water through forest soil into an underlying aquifer.

**photosynthesis** A series of biochemical reactions through which plants use chlorophyll and other light-absorbing pigments to transform carbon dioxide and water into carbohydrates and molecular oxygen with the energy derived from visible light.

**rotation** The period of time required for timber regeneration between successive timber harvests.

**salvage logging** Commercial removal of diseased, dead, damaged, or dying timber.

**second growth** A forest or timber stand that has regenerated following logging of the natural forest.

**seed tree cut**  A cut in which all but a few trees are removed, leaving only these few trees chosen for their superior quality and thinly dispersed over the logging site to provide seed for the next generation. Once the new trees have become established, the seed trees themselves are cut.

**selective cut**  A cut in which a few trees are chosen from a forest for removal according to specific criteria, such as age, size, quality, or species.

**shelterwood cut**  A modified clearcut very similar to a seed tree cut but with more trees left standing to shelter the next generation. Once the newly seeded trees have become established, the overstory trees are removed.

**silvics**  The study of the life histories and characteristics of forest trees, especially as influenced by environmental factors.

**silviculture**  The branch of forestry concerned with controlling the establishment, growth, reproduction, and care of forest trees for commercial use.

**soil seed bank**  The accumulation of seeds, fruits, and propagules (portions of a plant capable of developing into a complete plant) found in or on the soil, even after removal of trees or other vegetation.

**stomata**  Microscopic pores on the leaf cuticles of a plant that control the amount and rate of water vapor released from the plant as well as the exchange of oxygen and carbon dioxide.

**succession**  A predictable sequence of changes in species composition and structure over time in response to disturbance.

**sustained yield**  The amount of timber and other forest products and services that can be continuously produced in perpetuity from a forest or stand managed for timber production without degradation. More narrowly, a volume of timber cut but replaced by new forest growth in the period between cuts.

**taiga** A type of northern coniferous forest found south of the arctic tundra.

**timber stand improvement** Activities such as precommercial thinning, commercial thinning, brush control, and pesticide and herbicide applications, designed to improve the quality and quantity of timber produced.

**vector** A mobile species—such as an aphid carrying a plant virus—capable of transmitting a pathogen from one host to another; also any organism harboring the pathogen during a phase of its life cycle.

**water bar** An earthen ridge or other erosion-control structure (such as a wooden beam embedded in or staked in sloping ground) positioned, for example, across a hilly road, to divert water off to the side.

**watercourse** Any stream or streambed capable of moving water and associated sediment and debris.

**watershed** The expanse of land from which water flows into a water body; a drainage basin.

**water table** The below-ground level at which the soil or rock is saturated with water.

**windthrow** The uprooting of a tree by wind, or a tree so uprooted.

**yarding** Skidding, dragging, or otherwise moving a log from its stump to a loading area or truck.

# RECOMMENDED READING

*Books of special interest have been marked with an asterisk (\*).*

Alverson, William S.; Kuhlmann, Walter; and Waller, Donald M. 1994. *Wild Forests: Conservation Biology and Public Policy.* Washington, DC: Island Press.

Banuri, Tariq, and Marglin, Frederique Apffel, eds. 1993. *Who Will Save the Forests? Knowledge, Power and Environmental Destruction.* London: Zed Books.

Berger, John J. 1985. "Redwoods Rising." In *Restoring the Earth: How Americans Are Working to Renew Our Damaged Environment.* New York: Alfred A. Knopf.

Berger, John J., ed. 1990. *Environmental Restoration: Science and Strategies for Restoring the Earth.* Washington, DC: Island Press.

Caufield, Catherine. 1985. *In the Rainforest.* New York: Alfred A. Knopf.

Chase, Alston. 1995. *In a Dark Wood: The Fight over Forests and the Rising Tyranny of Ecology.* Boston: Houghton Mifflin.

Cubbage, F. W. 1995. "Regulation of Private Forest Practices: What Rights, Which Policies?" *Journal of Forestry,* vol. 93, no. 6 (June), pp. 14–20.

Dana, Samuel Trask, and Fairfax, Sally K. 1980. *Forest and Range Policy*. New York: McGraw-Hill Book Company.

*Davis, Mary Byrd, ed. 1996. *Eastern Old Growth Forests: Prospects for Rediscovery and Recovery*. Washington, DC: Island Press.

*Devall, Bill. 1994. *Clearcut: The Tragedy of Industrial Forestry*. San Francisco: Sierra Club/Earth Island Press.

*Dudley, Nigel; Jeanrenaud, Jean-Paul; and Sullivan, Francis. 1995. *Bad Harvest? The Timber Trade and the Degradation of the World's Forests*. London: Earthscan Publications.

*Durning, Alan Thein. 1993. *Saving the Forests: What Will It Take?* Washington, DC: Worldwatch Institute.

Ehrlich, Paul, and Ehrlich, Anne. 1981. *Extinction: The Causes and Consequences of the Disappearance of Species*. New York: Random House.

*Fazio, James R. 1985. *The Woodland Steward*. Moscow, ID: Woodland Press.

Food and Agriculture Organization of the United Nations. 1993. *Forestry Statistics Today for Tomorrow*. Rome.

*Forest Watch*. 1990. "America's Forests, The Graphic Facts." vol. 11, no. 5 (November/December), pp. 20–25.

*Forest Watch*. 1991. *The Citizen's Guide to the Timber Industry*, vol. 12, no. 1 (July).

Fox, Stephen. 1981. *John Muir and His Legacy: The American Conservation Movement*. Boston: Little, Brown and Company.

Franklin, Jerry F. 1995. "Scientists in Wonderland: Experiences in Development of Forest Policy." *Bioscience* (supplement, August), pp. 74–78.

Gradwohl, Judith, and Greenberg, Russell. 1988. *Saving the Tropical Forests*. Washington, DC: Island Press.

Guha, Ramachandra. 1993. "The Malign Encounter: The Chipko Movement and Competing Visions of Nature." In *Who Will Save the Forests? Knowledge, Power and Environmental Destruction,* edited by Tariq Banuri and Frederique Apffel Marglin. London: Zed Books.

*Hammond, Herb. 1991. *Seeing the Forest among the Trees: The Case for Wholistic Forest Use.* Vancouver, BC: Polestar Press.

Hardt, R. A., and Newman, D. H. 1995. "Regional Policies for National Forest Old-Growth Planning." *Journal of Forestry,* vol. 93, no. 6 (June), pp. 32–35.

Henning, Daniel H., and Mangun, William R. 1989. *Managing the Environmental Crisis.* Durham, NC: Duke University Press.

*Herndon, Grace. 1991. *Cut & Run: Saying Goodbye to the Last Great Forests in the West.* Telluride, CO: Western Eye Press.

Hirt, Paul W. 1994. *A Conspiracy of Optimism: Management of the National Forests since World War Two.* Lincoln: University of Nebraska Press.

Institute for Sustainable Forestry. 1994. *Pacific Certified Ecological Forest Products Landowner and Forester Handbook.* Redway, CA.

Institute for Sustainable Forestry. 1996. *Working Your Woods: An Introductory Guide to Sustainable Forestry.* Redway, CA.

Jordan, Richard. 1994. *Trees and People: Forestland, Ecosystems and Our Future.* Washington, DC: Regnery Publishing.

Kelly, Brian, and London, Mark. 1983. *Amazon.* New York: Harcourt Brace Jovanovich.

Kimmins, Hamish. 1992. *Balancing Act: Environmental Issues in Forestry.* Vancouver, BC: University of British Columbia Press.

MacCleery, Douglas W. 1991. "A Forest Retrospective." *Forest Watch,* vol. 12, no. 2 (September), pp. 20–25.

MacCleery, Douglas W. 1994. "Resiliency and Recovery: A Brief History of Conditions and Trends in U.S. Forests." *Forest & Conservation History,* June, pp. 135–39.

MacCleery, Douglas W. 1996. *American Forests: A History of Resiliency and Recovery.* Rev. ed. Durham, NC: Forest History Society.

MacDougall, A. Kent. 1987. "Worldwide Costs Mount as Trees Fall"; "Need for Wood Forestalled Conservation"; "Drought, Floods, Erosion Add to Impact of Tree Loss"; "Forest Reclamation: Last Resort after Conservation." *Los Angeles Times,* 14, 17, 19, and 22 June (four-part series).

MacLean, Jayne T. 1991. *Herbicides, Ecological Effects: January 1985–September 1991.* QB 92-06. Quick Bibliography Series. Alternative Farming Systems, Beltsville, MD: National Agricultural Library.

Margolin, Malcolm. 1985. *The Earth Manual: How to Work on Wild Land Without Taming It.* Berkeley, CA: Heyday Books.

*Maser, Chris. 1994. *Sustainable Forestry: Philosophy, Science, and Economics.* Del Ray Beach, FL: Saint Lucie Press.

Meyers, Norman. 1995. "The World's Forests: Need for a Policy Appraisal." *Science,* 12 May, pp. 823–34.

Mitchell, John G. 1991. *Dispatches from the Deep Woods.* Lincoln: University of Nebraska Press.

Naar, Jon. 1990. *Design for a Livable Planet.* New York: Harper & Row Publishers.

*Naar, Jon, and Naar, Alex J. 1992. *This Land Is Your Land: A Guide to North America's Endangered Ecosystems.* New York: HarperCollins Publishers.

Nemetz, Peter N., ed. 1992. *Emerging Issues in Forest Policy.* Vancouver, BC: University of British Columbia Press.

Noss, Reed F., and Cooperider, Allen Y. 1994. *Saving Nature's Legacy: Protecting and Restoring Biodiversity.* Washington, DC: Island Press.

Pavlik, Bruce M.; Muick, Pamela C.; Johnson, Sharon; and Popper, Marjorie. 1991. *Oaks of California.* Los Olivos, CA: Cachuma Press/California Oak Foundation.

Perlin, John. 1989. *A Forest Journey: The Role of Wood in the Development of Civilization.* New York: W. W. Norton and Company.

Peterken, George F. 1993. *Woodland Conservation and Mangement.* 2d ed. London: Chapman & Hall.

*Pilarski, Michael, ed. 1994. *Restoration Forestry: An International Guide to Sustainable Forestry Practices.* Durango, CO: Kivaki Press.

Preston, B. B. 1995. "Forestry in the 104th Congress: Political Winds in America's Forestlands." *Journal of Forestry,* vol. 93, no. 6 (June), pp. 4–7.

*Raphael, Ray. 1982. *Tree Talk.* Washington, DC: Island Press.

*Raphael, Ray. 1994. *More Tree Talk.* Washington, DC: Island Press.

*Robinson, Gordon. 1988. *The Forest and the Trees: A Guide to Excellent Forestry.* Washington, DC: Island Press.

Steelquist, Robert. 1992. "Salmon & Forests: Fog Brothers." *American Forests,* July–August.

Ulrich, Alice. 1990. *U.S. Timber Production, Trade, Consumption, and Price Statistics 1960–1988.* Misc. publ. no. 1486. Washington, DC: USDA, Forest Service.

U.S. Department of Agriculture. 1995. *Report of the Forest*

*Service. Fiscal Year 1994.* Washington, DC: USDA, Forest Service.

West, Terry L. 1991. *Centennial Mini-Histories of the Forest Service.* Washington, DC: USDA, Forest Service.

Wilderness Society. 1988. *National Forests: Policies for the Future.* Vols. 1–4. Washington, DC: Author.

Wilderness Society; Sierra Club; Natural Resources Defense Council; National Audubon Society; and National Wildlife Federation. 1983. *National Forest Planning: A Conservationist's Guide.* Washington, DC: Wilderness Society.

World Rainforest Movement. 1990. *Rainforest Destruction: Causes, Effects and False Solutions.* Penang, Malaysia.

World Resources Institute; United Nations Environment Programme; and United Nations Development Programme. 1994. "Forests and Rangelands." In *World Resources 1994–1995: A Guide to the Global Environment.* New York: Oxford University Press.

Zuckerman, Seth. 1991. *Saving Our Ancient Forests.* Los Angeles: Living Planet Press.

# INDEX

# About the Author

JOHN J. BERGER is an author and consultant specializing in natural resources, energy, and the environment. His books include *Restoring the Earth: How Americans Are Working to Renew Our Damaged Environment* and other volumes listed at the front of this book. He has served as a special consultant on environmental restoration science and policy to the National Research Council of the National Academy of Sciences and as a consultant on restoration ecology to the Office of Technology Assessment of the U.S. Congress. He holds a master's degree in energy and natural resources (University of California, Berkeley) and a Ph.D. in ecology (University of California, Davis), and has been a professor of environmental policy at the University of Maryland's Graduate School of Public Affairs. His popular writing has appeared in publications such as *Omni, Sierra, Audubon,* the *Los Angeles Times,* and the *Boston Globe.* He has worked extensively in the nonprofit as well as the commercial sector and currently can be reached at LSA Associates, Inc., 157 Park Place, Point Richmond, CA 94801, (510) 231-7714, or by e-mail at hfws90a@ prodigy.com. He lives in El Cerrito, California. ✥